NORTHAN
TALES OF
& MUKDER

Other areas covered in this series include:

Berkshire
Buckinghamshire
Cheshire
Cornwall
Derbyshire
Devon
East Anglia
Essex
Hampshire
Hertfordshire
Kent
Lancashire
Leicestershire and Rutland
Lincolnshire
Middlesex
Nottinghamshire
Somerset
Staffordshire
Surrey
Sussex
Warwickshire
Wiltshire

Northamptonshire
· Tales of ·

David Saint

COUNTRYSIDE BOOKS
NEWBURY BERKSHIRE

First published 2005
© David Saint 2005

COUNTRYSIDE BOOKS
3 Catherine Road
Newbury, Berkshire

To view our complete range of books,
please visit us at
www.countrysidebooks.co.uk

ISBN 1 85306 945 0
EAN 978 1 85306 945 1

Cover designed by Peter Davies,
Nautilus Design

Produced through MRM Associates Ltd., Reading
Typeset by Mac Style Ltd, Scarborough, N. Yorkshire
Printed by Borcombe Printers, Romsey

Contents

MAP OF NORTHAMPTONSHIRE

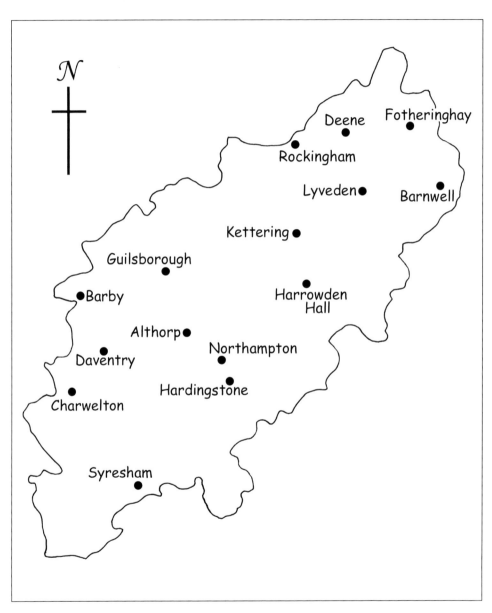

Introduction

Like many clergymen, I have always loved reading murder mysteries. Miss Marple and Hercule Poirot have been constant travelling companions of mine when I have holidayed abroad and yet, when I came to look at some of the real murders and mysteries of my home county, Northamptonshire, it all seemed a little too close to home!

My journey through some of these murders and mysteries has taken me to some wonderful places in the county and on the way I have been helped by some remarkable people to whom I am immensely grateful.

The accounts that follow are about real people and, somehow, it was impossible not to share in their stories. For instance, I stood over the grave of Mary Jane Pursglove in Kettering's borough cemetery and felt almost part of her tragic life. Then, as I walked across present day Campbell Square in Northampton, it was hard to realise that it was there that young PC Kemp lost his life so pointlessly. His memorial in Billing Road cemetery remains ever poignant to me. In Hardingstone, the cross marking the grave of an unknown man seems mysteriously romantic until all the terrible and gruesome facts become known. And, because I was born in Daventry, the dreadful story of the Pinckard family had a special relevance to me.

I visited the small museum at Northamptonshire Police Headquarters at Wootton Hall in Northampton. I learned from the jovial and very helpful Richard Cowley that the museum is now a mere shadow of its former self. However, I was fascinated by the macabre birch rods once used to punish offenders in the county, until the 1948 Criminal Justice Act outlawed them. Then there was the bolt from a door in the old Northampton Gaol that stood on the site of the present Police HQ in Campbell Square. Built in 1847, the gaol was demolished in the 1920s. There is even a sword dating from 1868 that was used by police in rural areas, when footpads and other malingerers were abroad. Some of the items in the museum, which is open to the public every day, date from the times when many of the stories in this book took place.

The modern police force has far more sophisticated equipment with which to solve crimes and to protect themselves and the public. To Northamptonshire Police and to all other forces, we must give our utmost support and gratitude.

David Saint

Acknowledgements

My thanks go to: Colin Eaton, Terry Bracker and Hilary Miller, Northampton Libraries; staff at Kettering and Wellingborough Public Libraries; the Librarian at the *Northamptonshire Evening Telegraph*; Lay Canon Terence Cocks FSA, archivist, Leicester Cathedral; Richard Edgecumbe, Victoria and Albert Museum; Earl Spencer for permission to quote from his book, *Althorp, the Story of an English House*; Frances Domeny, Althorp; Emma Grayson, Mr and The Hon. Mrs Brudenell, Deene Park; John-Paul Carr, Wellingborough Heritage Centre; Betty Thompson and Clive Herbert, Guilsborough; Sue Williams, Kettering Borough Council Bereavement Services; Mark Bradshaw, the National Trust, Lyvedon New Bield; Peter Start and the Barby Historical Society; Richard Cowley, Northamptonshire Police; the Secretary, Wellingborough Golf Club; Paula, Jennie and Dawn; Trevor Rhodes for additional photographs and Dennis Wiles Cloves for endless support and for proof reading!

THE MICHAELMAS FAIR MURDER

——————— ❁ ———————

Daventry 1851

When I was a lad growing up in Daventry, we used to look forward to the one annual fair with great excitement and I can still recall the smells, the sounds and the disappointing prizes! It was held in October and was called 'The Mops'. The roundabouts and sideshows were a far cry from the original purpose of the Mops Fair, which was for the hiring of servants.

Up until the mid-19th century, Daventry held no less than thirteen fairs throughout each year. Most of them were for horses and cattle and an Act of Parliament strictly controlled what was sold at each fair. For example, the Michaelmas Fair lasted for two days and on the first day, only 'cheese, onions and all sorts of wares and merchandise' could be offered for sale but, on the second day, 'all sorts of beasts, horses, sheep and other cattle' were allowed. The penalty for breaking this law was 20 shillings for each and every offence.

The 20 shilling penalty for that transgression of the law was very small when compared with the penalty meted out to another transgressor of the law in Daventry in October 1851.

The Michaelmas Fair attracted crowds of people. There were those in the town who were regulars, but many of those who lived in the outlying villages would go only if they had a special reason. On 3rd October 1851, John Mutton Pinckard had a reason. He was going to take a horse to the fair to be sold. At 9 o'clock in the morning, he left his home at Lower Thrupp Grounds Farm and went to collect his father, Richard, for their day out. It was about $^3/_4$ mile along the road to Daventry from John's farm to his father's cottage.

John lived in the hope of getting a good price for the horse. He needed the money very badly, so badly in fact, that he would have sold almost anything, but his father was not aware of that.

Richard bade a fond farewell to his wife Elizabeth who, although she had been in hospital, was now in good health and had never been in better spirits. Once Richard had left with their son, Elizabeth set about preparing dinner ready for her husband's return.

Back at Lower Thrupp Grounds Farm, another Elizabeth Pinckard was also making preparations, but not for dinner. This Elizabeth was John's wife, and she was preparing something that she thought would be absolutely perfect. She had made the recipe up herself; she had nearly all the ingredients; and all she had to do now was finalise the method.

Elizabeth had a servant, Ann Cross. She was a good worker and, as a single woman, she had no one dependent on her so she 'lived in' at the farm. This morning Ann was busy sweeping the kitchen. At ten o'clock, Elizabeth asked her to go over to John Farr, the baker in Welton, to get some bread. It was not far to go, she could cut across the farmyard, through a field and onto the canal bridge. Then it was only about a mile to Mr Farr's. Elizabeth knew exactly how far it was and how long it would take Ann. Off Ann went, leaving Elizabeth alone in the house.

Just as Ann was leaving, the clock in the house struck ten. That was the exact time that one of John's farm labourers,

Thomas Hadland, saw Elizabeth cross the field in the direction of Daventry. She was wearing a light coloured dress with a shawl over her arm. He wasn't spying, of course, but he did happen to notice that she came back at about a quarter to twelve.

At ten to twelve, Ann arrived back at Lower Thrupp farmhouse with the bread. She'd been quite quick: Elizabeth had expected her to take two hours, but no matter. Elizabeth seemed a little agitated. As soon as Ann had shut the door Elizabeth opened it again and looked out. Ann put the bread away and was about to carry on with her jobs when she saw that her mistress had changed her clothes. Earlier she'd been wearing a light dress, now she had on a dark coloured lilac one. And what's more, this dress was torn at the gathers and hung down. When Ann remarked on this, Elizabeth explained that she had caught it on the key of the dairy door. She said that, while Ann was away, she had been blackberrying but she had eaten all she had gathered. Elizabeth went to the door again. In fact Ann was conscious that her mistress kept going to the door. Perhaps she was anxious about John. Perhaps she had some jobs for him to do and she was just checking to see if he was in the yard.

Ann and Elizabeth sat down in the kitchen to each a lunch of bread and cheese. Then Elizabeth went upstairs to change her dress. When she came back she sat down and started mending the lilac one. She told Ann that she might go to the fair, but she didn't.

Meanwhile, John and his father left the fair in Daventry to make their way home. A workmate of John's, Edward Major, had gone to the fair with them. They reached old Mr Pinckard's cottage at about a quarter to twelve. Edward Major went into the kitchen and saw Mrs Pinckard sitting in the corner of the room. He asked her for a glass of water, but she didn't answer. He noticed there was some cloth tape round her neck. He thought it all a bit strange and a little frightening, and, being a simple soul, he hurried out of the house and on to Lower Thrupp Grounds Farm as quickly as he could. As he ran, he heard Welton's church clock strike twelve.

As the afternoon wore on, Ann quietly finished her chores and Elizabeth her mending. Then the silence was broken as they heard someone at the kitchen door. Expecting to see her master, Ann was surprised to see John Letts, a farm labourer, standing in the doorway. He had a grave look on his face. Instinctively Ann thought the worst. Had her master been in an accident? But the news Letts brought was even worse. He came straight in and addressed Elizabeth. 'Your mother-in-law's dead. She's hung herself', he said.

After a few exchanges, Letts left. It was arranged that Ann should go and spend the night at the dead woman's cottage so that she could help and comfort old Richard Pinckard. She left Elizabeth making dumplings, of all things!

The next morning Ann came back to Lower Thrupp. Elizabeth said that she had washed her dress twice and asked Ann to go and turn it so that it would dry. Ann found that one of her own dresses had also been washed, which was exceptional, Elizabeth had never before washed one of Ann's dresses. She went outside and found the lilac dress drying on the hedge. Later, when she went to bed, she found the same dress hanging on her bedpost. Quite why it was there, she had no idea.

Matthew Sharman was one of three surgeons serving in Daventry. He shared premises with Mr Thompson and Mr Watts in Litchfield Street, now called New Street, just off the Market Square. At about 6 pm on 3rd October, he arrived at the cottage. He saw old Elizabeth Pinckard's body lying on its right side with the head on a pillow. The face was swollen and discoloured and there was a bruise over the right eye. There were wounds on the head to suggest a blow with a fairly large blunt instrument. There was some cloth tape around the neck and some more tape attached to a hook from the ceiling. Clearly death was not caused by strangulation alone, but in conjunction with the head wound. There was nothing to suggest that the deceased had taken her own life, indeed, everything suggested that she had been attacked and then strangled – the presence of smeared blood on the wall nearby clearly confirmed this.

If old Elizabeth Pinckard had not killed herself, who was responsible? On Sunday 5th October, Mr Sharman went to Lower Thrupp farmhouse and suggested to Elizabeth that her mother-in-law had been murdered. Elizabeth said she too was of that opinion and that whoever had done it should be caught and punished. She said that there was nobody who was at enmity with the deceased, indeed you could live and die with her and never have a cross word. Sharman said that somebody had been seen going to and from the cottage on the day of the murder. Elizabeth said that she had discussed the very matter with her husband and could make nothing of it.

On Monday 6th October, PC Edward Osborne was sent to speak to young Elizabeth Pinckard at Lower Thrupp Grounds Farm. He said to her, 'No doubt someone had done the deed that had an interest in it.' Elizabeth replied, 'I can assure you, sir, that I did not want to take Mrs Pinckard's life, or anybody else's for the sake of money. I had plenty of money at home.'

But she didn't have plenty of money at home; in fact she and her husband had no money anywhere. John had insured his life for £300 but that was of little use. They were in dire straits. Their landlord, Thomas Wathorne, had constantly reminded them that they were well in arrears with their rent. He had said that John Pinckard should have put money aside and that he, Wathorne, would not consider waiting a day longer. He reminded them that it would take a long time for them to complete the threshing of their corn and there would be no immediate income from that, so they had better ask a friend to help them pay the rent and then they could pay the friend back when the old lady died.

When the old lady died? What did he know? Was it common knowledge that John and Elizabeth Pinckard stood to inherit some money when old Elizabeth died? Perhaps everybody knew. But how? John had certainly never boasted about it, he and his wife had tried to give the impression to everyone that they were comfortably off. But the truth was very different.

John would be well off one day. His great uncle, Francis Mutton, had no children and, in his will, he had left £1,000 to his niece, John's mother, Elizabeth Pinckard. The will had been witnessed by an old, deaf man called Gibbins, and John had seen old Mr Mutton execute it. But John's mother had lived her 'three score and ten'. How long much longer must he wait? Not long, if his wife had anything to do with it.

And so it was. Young Elizabeth Pinckard had carefully planned it all. She knew that John had arranged with his father that they would go to the Michaelmas Horse Fair on 3rd October to sell the mare. She knew that it would take Ann two hours to go over to Farr's for the bread. She knew that the rest of the workers were well out of the way, occupied in jobs around the farm. She knew that her mother-in-law would be at home on her own. She had planned the crime perfectly. At least, she may have had the theory worked out, but she had failed in the practice – because she had been careless.

She took advantage of some tape from the old lady's sewing box and used it to strangle her. The old lady struggled, and so Elizabeth hit her on the head with a mallet that she had carried under her shawl. She tightened the tape again and, in order to make it look like suicide, looked for a ceiling hook from which to hang the dying woman. In the process, she smeared blood on the wall, but failed to notice it. She also failed to realise that the position in which she had left her mother-in-law was unconvincing.

She had been careless in not reckoning on Edward Major wanting a glass of water. She didn't reckon on John Liddington, another labourer who was working on the road, spotting her at 11.30 am leaving the Pinckard cottage in the direction of Lower Thrupp Grounds Farm. Or that William Cole had seen her go into the cottage. Or that William Reynolds, a local bobby, on his way to Daventry Fair, would see her actually standing at the door of the cottage at about 11.30 am. Or that three or four other people, who knew her well, would see her at that time either going to, or leaving the cottage.

She had been careless. She should not have worn the dress she had ripped on that dreadful morning. She should not have admitted to washing her dress twice and involving Ann Cross in helping to dry it. And why did she wash Ann's dress anyway? And why was Elizabeth's dress hanging in Ann's bedroom? She should not have made up the story about picking blackberries and eating them all.

All very careless. And very stupid. And very, very evil.

At the end of her trial, in February 1852, Elizabeth Pinckard showed no emotion whatsoever. And even less, when Judge Jervis addressed her from beneath his black cap.

'A Jury of your country have been compelled to perform the painful duty of pronouncing you guilty of murder, of murder which at all times black and dreadful, becomes in your case doubly black and dreadful. You have hurried, without a moment's warning out of the world a poor creature with whom, according to your own account, you might have lived and died without a cross word.'

THE YELLOW MERCEDES-BENZ AND THE NAZI SPY

❊

Guilsborough 1939

Not long ago, a 1937 yellow Mercedes-Benz turned up in a London dealer's. It was admired by all who saw it, because it had been looked after remarkably well and was a perfect example of a car of its age. But few who saw the gleaming car in the showroom realised that it had a mysterious and fascinating history. It had been given up by its original owner rather quickly just before the declaration of the Second World War, since when it had been bought and cherished by several careful owners.

In 1939, it was just as much of an eye-catcher as it drove around the country lanes of Northamptonshire. At the wheel was a dashing young man with his glamorous lady-love at his side. They had come to live in Guilsborough, a beautiful village of golden sandstone that had become a Mecca for members a select and wealthy social set.

The area around Guilsborough is fine hunting country; Pytchley Hunt country. For hundreds of years, it has attracted the rich, the famous and the titled from all over the world. It was known to high society as 'The cream of the cream in the shire of the shires'; a sobriquet that would hold little credence nowadays. In the 19th century, the Empress Elizabeth of Austria rented Cottesbrooke Hall and took Northamptonshire by storm. In the 1920s, Nancy Tree came from Virginia and lived at Kelmarsh Hall with her husband, the Master of the Pytchley. In the 1930s, The Duke and Duchess of York had a number of seasons in the county and lived in various country houses known as 'hunting boxes', in Naseby, Thornby, and Guilsborough. The Duke of Windsor learned to hunt from Pitsford Hall and indeed Queen Elizabeth II as a girl, first hunted in Northamptonshire.

In the 1930s, country life was in its heyday with lots of hunting and point-to-points by day and parties by night. So when the new and very elegant couple from Europe arrived, they fitted in with most of the smart set. But not all.

Thirty four-year-old Herr Von Treck and his companion, Baroness Violet Schroder, appeared to have all the requirements for the English country life: breeding, style and wealth. But in the mid to late thirties there was still resentment amongst those of the local gentry who had memories of the First World War and also those who were

Guilsborough House.

beginning to understand the political implications of events across the English Channel. No one knew anything about the newcomers, apart from the fact that they were German.

Von Treck and his baroness made every effort to be accepted. They bought historic Guilsborough House, which dates from 1632, and they stayed there for two years during which time Von Treck lived the life of a gentleman. He had a butler, a footman, a stud groom, five strappers and a driver-mechanic called Mr Wagstaff to look after his yellow Mercedes. Money was no object and the house rang to wild and extravagant dinner parties as the couple entertained their new-found friends.

By day, the baroness stayed at home, but Von Treck rode to hounds with incredible energy and regularity, not only with the Pytchley, but also with other local hunts, the Belvoir and the Fernie. Thus, he grew to know the countryside extremely well. Too well as it turned out. For from the saddle, Von Treck was not merely admiring the undulating Northamptonshire countryside, he was taking a keen but covert interest in some other activity that was beginning to take hold in the county.

In the late 1930s, much to the annoyance of the hunting fraternity, new military airfields were being built. In Northamptonshire alone there were eighteen and, remarkably, within a gallop from Guilsborough there were a dozen including Desborough, Chipping Warden, Deenthorpe, Grafton Underwood, Harrington, King's Cliffe, Polebrook, Spanhoe and Sywell.

As others on horseback complained about the work on the airfields that interrupted their sport and forced unnecessary diversions, Herr Von Treck, with nodding mock agreement, took more than a passing interest in the emerging layout. Herr Von Treck had been sent to England to spy for Nazi Germany and he undertook his espionage without rousing the slightest suspicion. He gathered his information by day and collated it by night in meticulously assembled files concealed in Guilsborough House. Then, on the instructions of his superiors, after two years of 'hunting', Von Treck's life as a sporting gentleman in Northamptonshire came to an end.

At 11 o'clock on 3rd September 1939, war was declared between Britain and Germany. In the last week of August, Herr Von Treck and Baroness Violet Schroder, with carefully packed suitcases in the boot, drove away from Guilsborough House for the last time in the yellow Mercedes. The members of staff were paid off and the house was left fully furnished, and the Von Trecks left England via Northold airport. Within weeks the house was placed under the custodianship of the Trustees of Enemy Alien Property. Von Treck had given his yellow Mercedes to his driver, Mr Wagstaff, but it was never seen in Guilsborough again.

An auction of Von Treck's remaining property was held at Guilsborough House soon after he 'disappeared'. Mr Wagstaff found alternative employment in a local garage but was restricted to the village during the remaining years of the war by police security regulations. The groom, Eddie Phelan, who coincidentally had a German wife, went to work at Weedon Ordnance Depot. However, his employment was terminated abruptly once details of his former employer were released, but neither he nor his wife was interned.

And so it would seem that the strange tale of Guilsborough's German spy ends there. But, in fact, the story has a mysterious conclusion.

In an ironic twist worthy of fiction, Guilsborough House was taken over by the War Office shortly after Von Treck left. The man in charge was Major General Sir Evelyn Dalrymple Fanshawe who amazingly lived literally down the road at Nortoft House, also in Guilsborough. General Fanshawe knew Von Treck, of course, for both were very much part of the hunting fraternity. 'Neither Colonel Lowther nor I normally accepted his invitations, being acidly polite', Fanshawe later recorded, adding that he accepted only one invitation to dinner with the German; he preferred to keep his distance.

One day General Fanshawe was summoned to the War Office in London to be interviewed by the Minister of War, Leslie Hore-Belisha. Fanshawe was to be promoted and put in charge of armoured development, drawing together seven yeomanry regiments ranging from the Fife and Forfars to the London based Sharpshooters and including the Northamptonshire Yeomanry. Belisha asked him where he would like to establish his headquarters. Since the task ranged nationwide, Fanshawe suggested Guilsborough House. And so the house was given a strategic wartime purpose and was requisitioned in effect from Herr Von Treck!

Subsequently Guilsborough House became the final headquarters of almost every armoured division in the British Army. It played an important part in the fight against Nazi Germany.

But still the story is not complete!

In the summer of 1945, soon after the end of the war, General Fanshawe was serving as a refugee organiser for the United Nations. One day he had a telephone call from General Charles Hayden. 'I say, Evelyn, do you remember a fellow called Treck hunting with the Pytchley? I want to talk to you about him.' When the two soldiers met, General Fanshawe was told that Von Treck had been caught in Germany, but someone was needed to go over to identify him. 'Will you do it?' General Hayden clearly had no idea of the extraordinary connection between Fanshawe and his quarry.

General Fanshawe returned to Guilsborough and to the house in which Von Treck had collated so much of his espionage material. A day or so later, he was driven to southern Germany where he came face to face, once more, with the man at whose table he had dined just once. But this was no social meeting; it was a matter of national security. By now, Von Treck had been underground for some time and had grown a beard. That did not prevent General Fanshawe from recognising him instantly. 'That's him', he said and Von Treck was taken into custody. The files he had accumulated while on his 'hunting' exploits in Northamptonshire revealed just how much of a threat his work had been to Great Britain during those dark years of war.

To round things off, Major General Evelyn Dalrymple Fanshawe and his beloved wife bought Guilsborough House and lived in it for many years. From it General Fanshawe regularly continued to hunt – but not for spies!

THE GHOST IN THE ROYAL GARDEN

———— ❀ ————

Barnwell Manor 1941

When I was a boy playing with toy soldiers, I longed to have a castle. In those days, every lad's dream of a real castle was of a four-square stronghold with a big stone turret at each of the four corners, and an entrance with a moat and drawbridge.

Barnwell Castle in Northamptonshire is just such a castle. In fact, when Berengar le Moyne built it in 1266, it was the English prototype of that very thing, the toy-town castle! It was the first example anywhere in Britain of what Pevsner in his *Buildings of Northamptonshire* calls, 'The most monumental type of castle architecture'. Even now, all these hundreds of years later, Barnwell Castle still looks impressive and impenetrable. It stands in the grounds of Barnwell Manor, home since the 1930s to the Dukes of Gloucester. And it is in the grounds of the manor, very near to the castle, that the late Princess Alice, Duchess of Gloucester, had a strange and mysterious experience. It is a story well known in Barnwell village, a community of which the Princess was a much-loved part.

Royalty have long regarded Northamptonshire as an ideal home. It is the county in which William the Conqueror built his mighty Rockingham Castle; King Edward and Queen

Barnwell Castle (Reproduced by permission of Northamptonshire Libraries and Information Service).

Eleanor often came to their royal lodges at Kings Cliffe and Geddington and stayed, for official business, at Northampton Castle. Countless parliaments and royal councils have been held here; Richard III was born here and Queen Mary of Scotland died here. In more modern times, the late Queen Mother, as Duchess of York, spent a great deal of time hunting around Guilsborough and Naseby. It is, in every sense, a royal county.

The Gloucesters made their home at Barnwell in 1938 when Prince Henry, 3rd son of King George V and Queen Mary, married Lady Alice Montagu-Douglas-Scott. She was a daughter of the Duke of Buccleuch and Queensbury, who has his most glorious home at Boughton House, just ten miles away from Barnwell.

The young Duchess of Gloucester very soon established herself as a jewel in the life of Northamptonshire and as the Second World War approached, she made herself available to any charitable cause that needed her support. Very close to Barnwell were several American airbases: Deenthorpe,

Polebrook and also Grafton Underwood, which was actually on the family's estate at Boughton.

Polebrook airfield was just a few miles up the road from Barnwell on land belonging to Princess Alice's good friend, the late Dame Miriam Rothschild. At its height, the airfield was home to 6,000 US Airmen including, at one point, Clark Gable and James Stewart! In their off-duty hours, the airmen enjoyed the rural life of Northamptonshire, with its typically English villages so loved by visitors from abroad.

Princess Alice noted in her diary for 1941 that, on one occasion, her husband, Prince Henry, was due to land at Polebrook on his return from a diplomatic mission to India and the Middle East. He was eager to see his new son and heir, Prince William. Since Prince Henry was arriving unexpectedly, a hurriedly coded message had been sent in order to secure his safe arrival. Unfortunately it was also the same time that Clark Gable was due to fly in for his period of service on the base. The press had gathered at the airfield in order to get pictures of 'Mr Hollywood' and so there was a certain degree of excitement on the tarmac. When the door of the plane opened and Prince Henry stepped out, the paparazzi put their cameras away and grumbled, 'Oh no, it's not him!' And they went away for a cup of tea and a cigarette.

Later in the same year Princess Alice, again in her diary, noted that she looked out of her drawing room window to see about fifty Americans having their photographs taken against the Castle walls, quite uninvited. She didn't really mind since, for some time, she had let it be known that her beautiful gardens were always open to the American airmen to visit freely.

There was one regular visitor who came so often that Princess Alice began to recognise him. He was young, fair-haired and very pleasant. So regular was he that the Princess allowed him the singular privilege of picking strawberries if

HRH Princess Alice with author on the occasion of her 80th birthday.

he felt so inclined! He had clearly found something of a spiritual home at Barnwell; it is quite easy to leave your soul in a place as beautiful as Barnwell's gardens, personally designed and tended by the late Princess herself.

Then one day, Princess Alice was in a hurry and was rushing back to the house to give Prince William his bath. As she passed the old castle walls, near to where the strawberries grew in profusion, it was no surprise at all when she saw her friendly young American.

'Can I look around again, Ma'am?' He must have had a smile as wide as the Golden Gate Bridge; he was friendly and always polite to the Princess.

'Of course', she agreed and thought nothing of it. She shouted her reply over her shoulder and carried on across the lawns. As she ran, she turned to look again and to smile a kind of apology for her unseemly haste. But as she turned, the airman was not there. Maybe he had scooted round the castle to the strawberries.

A few days later, when some other American airmen came to the gardens, they had a sad look on their faces. Princess Alice, with her usual concern, asked if anything was the matter. As the airmen told her their news, Princess Alice, the most composed and dignified lady imaginable, froze.

It seems that on the very day that she saw her fair-haired young American, he had been shot down and killed on a bombing mission over Germany.

THE GREEN DOOR OF JEALOUSY

———————— ❁ ————————

Kettering 1912

In 1901, the second Boer War was raging. Names like Mafeking and Ladysmith, Spion Kop and Diamond Hill would become familiar through the daily reports in the newspapers. Heroes like Baden Powell and Kitchener inspired hope and pride in the men who were fighting so many miles away.

A young soldier called Arthur Pursglove was caught up in that bitter war. In 1895 he had married his sweetheart, Mary, and they had found a home in Northampton. Arthur and Mary were never well off, and the poor young bride knew that, at anytime, Arthur could be called away to rejoin his regiment. Soon after they married, their daughter, Elizabeth Mary, was born and then, in 1898, a son Harry was born. Another mouth to feed, another child to clothe. So it was tragic when, after only six years together, Arthur and Mary found that their marriage was not as happy as they first thought. He was forced to spend time away with the army, leaving Mary at home with their children, and she simply could not cope. Although she could have managed on a soldier's pay, she had a weakness – she fell into the habit of spending more money on drink than on food and clothing for herself, Elizabeth and Harry.

By 1901, the marriage was all but over. Arthur, ashamed of his wife's behaviour and lack of care, walked out. He rejoined his regiment and sailed back to South Africa. The War was nearly over and negotiations for peace between Britain and the Boers were well under way. Arthur's fate is not known, but what is certain, is that he never returned to Kettering and he never saw Mary and his children again.

Mary had no real feelings of loss over Arthur. She was resigned to his absence; if he were found to be dead, that would have been a satisfactory resolution to the situation. She wanted a new life. In 1902, she moved to Kettering, where her mother was already living, and she even went so far as to change her name. Instead of reverting to her maiden name, Mary Hayden, chose the name Pittam and lived as a widow. It was easy to pretend that her brave soldier husband had died in some fierce battle in the Boer War, and a sure way of getting sympathy.

Arthur was quickly forgotten and pretty soon Mary had paired up with another man, Frank Bell. Together they moved to a hovel in Carrington Street, where a daughter, Gladys, was born. Bell was an engine driver on the Midland Railway. He was a steady man with a steady job and a steady income. Everything should have been rosy for Mary and her family.

But Mary's wanton streak would not let her settle down. She had tired of Arthur, now she tired of Frank, and it was not long before she had turned her attention to yet another man, a year her junior.

She met Isaac Edward Sewell, known to one and all as Ted, in her local pub, the Wagon and Horses. Ted was 35 and came from Pytchley, a village a couple of miles out of Kettering. For years he had helped his father in his work as a carrier, collecting and delivering goods between Pytchley, Kettering and the surrounding villages. When his father died, Ted took over the business, but he had grown bored with it and had left it for his two brothers to run while he found work in a shoe factory in Kettering.

Just before Christmas in 1910, Mary left Frank Bell and moved in with Ted Sewell. They found a place in Gas Street where they lived as a family with Mary's three children. Mary's eldest daughter, Elizabeth, was now old enough to get married and start a life of her own, but she stayed at home and carried on working as a shoe machinist. She would be giving up work soon anyway, because she was about to have a child.

As far as Ted was concerned it was a new relationship and a new home, a new start and a new life. But not for Mary. Her time with Bell had meant more to her than she realised and deep down she still carried a candle for him, but of course, that was something she would never have told Ted.

In June 1912, Ted Sewell heard of a house going for rent, near to the factory where he worked. He had been employed by Mobbs Bros. in Northall Street for some time and the house was only a few doors away. It seemed perfect. The house, though, was no dream home. Northall Street, stuck between Rockingham Road and Rothwell Road, was one of the poorest areas of Kettering. The house was a typical 'two up, two down', with a door onto the street, but it did have one advantage, there was a long stretch of allotments behind that lay between it and Tanners Lane. So it had a bit of green space nearby, somewhere for the children to play. The neighbours were kind and friendly, and Mary had made a special friend of Sarah Smith, an older, matronly woman from number 79.

But all was not well. By now, Mary's daughter, Elizabeth had given birth to her baby. In order to supplement money provided by the putative father, Mary had agreed to help out with a weekly sum towards the child's maintenance. This further drain on the household's finances caused more than a little tension. Indeed, it was the cause of frequent rows that were overheard by half the neighbourhood. Both Mary and Ted had quick, fiery tempers, fuelled by their regular drinking. Whenever these rows started, Ted left and went to the pub. More often than not, Mary went somewhere else for solace – to Carrington Street and to the bed of Frank Bell.

Before Ted came along, Bell's relationship with Mary had been good, and he hated it when she went off with a rival. Men like Bell don't like being dumped by a woman and, worse, the fact that Mary came to see him 'on the quiet' was no way to carry on. He resented being a convenient shoulder to cry on. He had shared his life, in fact everything, with her and he wanted it to be the same again, but it was clear that he was nothing to her and that made him angry. By now he knew what Mary was like, she was obviously playing him off against Ted. So what should he do? Tell her he never wanted to see her again? Or find some way of putting and end to the whole sordid affair so that he could get on with his life.

Word of Mary's unfaithfulness got round, and within weeks, Ted learned about her visits to Frank Bell. But Mary was careless; she and her neighbour, Sarah Smith, talked a lot and confided in each other. Mary made no secret of the fact that had been seeing a string of men over the years and, further, she admitted than none of them had been, what could be called, 'perfect gentlemen'! They were all hard workers, heavy drinkers and possessive. Possessive to the point of violence.

On 27th July, just five weeks after they moved into their cottage in Northall Street, Mary and Ted were on good terms, but it was a day that changed everything. In the afternoon, Mary said she was going out shopping, leaving Ted with Elizabeth and Gladys. Her thirteen-year-old son Harry was away in St John's Reform School at Tiffield, near Towcester. When Mary returned, she and Ted had another

Mary Jane Pursglove and Isaac Edward Sewell.

of their blazing rows and he made terrifying threats to her.
'If you've been with Bell any more, I'll bloody well do for
you.'

'I haven't been with anybody,' Mary screamed. She went
on to say that she had had enough, 'If you do not leave my
house, I shall. I am not going to have my life threatened, and
it's not the first time you have said it to me.'

Ted went out.

At about 2 pm, Elizabeth left the house with her new baby
and went to the Pytchley Feast celebrations. Young Gladys
went off with her friends to play. It was a hot day and, in a
small house with so many people, tempers can become
frayed at the best of times. It was better that everyone had a
little room to breathe.

The afternoon passed. Evening came. Elizabeth was still
out and Gladys was still playing. Ted was walking in the

town centre and just as the clock of St Peter and St Paul's church chimed 7 pm, he bumped into Catherine Hayden, Mary's mother. They didn't get on but Ted stopped her and said that he had something to tell her. Cath was in a hurry and, anyway, she didn't want to hear anything from him.

Ted then went for a drink in the Three Cocks. He asked for two-pennyworth of whisky. 'He seemed like a man in a hurry to catch a train', Bill Coleman the landlord said later. Ted asked for a drop of water for his whisky, he drank it and went away in the direction of the High Street. His next stop was the Old White Horse where he met a drinking partner, seventeen-year-old Joseph Saddington, who asked Ted to have a drink. Ted said, 'I'll have a drink and then go along the street. I'll see you later', and, after ten minutes, Ted left.

But where did he go?

At 8.30 pm, Ted saw one of his workmates, Len Essam, and together they went back to the Old White Horse. By now Ted was much the worse for drink, and the landlord refused to serve him. Len offered to take Ted home with him, but Ted, rather strangely said, 'No, you won't see me down Northall no more.' Len told him not to talk silly, to which Ted replied, 'You won't see me any more after tonight.' Len asked if he was going abroad. 'You don't know what I know,' was Ted's equally enigmatic reply. Then at a few minutes past nine, Ted kissed Len and said, 'Goodbye, I shan't see you no more.'

While all this was happening, young Gladys had finished playing and was ready to go home. She went to the green front door and tried to open it but found it locked. Her immediate thought was that her mother and Ted had gone out for a drink, so she went round to number 79 to ask Mrs Smith to help her get into the house. Sarah Smith and Gladys went back to 76 and found both the front and back doors locked, so Sarah pushed Gladys through the open front window. A moment later, Sarah heard terrible screams as Gladys hurled herself down the staircase and unlocked the door from the inside and let Sarah in. She ran upstairs to the back bedroom. What she saw would stay with her for the rest of her life.

In the shadows of the summer evening, Sarah saw Mary lying, fully clothed on the bed. Sarah lit a candle so that she could see more clearly. Mary's left leg was slightly drawn up, her right arm was across her neck. Her throat had been cut and blood was dripping through the bedclothes. On the floor were a shoemaker's knife and a green cap.

Sarah rushed Gladys from the house and raised the alarm. Within minutes the police and a doctor had arrived.

After he had uncharacteristically kissed Len Essam on the cheek and bid him a drunken farewell, Ted staggered to Wadcroft, where Mary's mother, Catherine Hayden, lived. As she opened the door to him, he collapsed in the passage and passed out.

Cath Hayden was having none of it. Ted had already threatened her and had made strong allegations about Mary and she wasn't having him on her floor all night. She called a policeman. PC Taylor, who was on the corner of Wadcroft at that moment, managed to get Ted to his feet and dragged him the short distance to the police station. After the briefest of formalities, because of Ted's stupor, PC Taylor and duty Inspector Dunn dumped Ted into a cell.

As the two officers turned to leave, Ted supported himself against the wall and started to use the lavatory in the corner of the cell. As he did so he murmured audibly words that stopped the two men in their tracks.

'I have murdered a girl tonight. I cut her bloody head off. You needn't trouble. I know I'll hang.'

Ted was too drunk to be charged with anything but, before they left him in the cell, the officers went through his pockets. They found very little: a few coins, a handkerchief and a key.

Ted Sewell came from a large family. His father had died 23 years earlier and his mother had since married again. He had three brothers and three sisters and one of the brothers had been an imbecile from birth. According to the medical reports, two of Ted's uncles had committed suicide within the past five years. People in Pytchley who knew the family thought Ted had peculiar habits too. "Is it any wonder," they'd said?

Folk had remembered that in May 1908, while Ted was cycling along Market Street, he had been involved in an accident. He was taken to the hospital where they found he was suffering from concussion. His brother, Jim, said that Ted had fractured both his jaw and his skull and was off work for over a month and drew money from the club. A year later he started work at Mobbs shoe factory. Workmates recalled that on many occasions Ted had complained of terrible headaches and had said he wanted to die and, on one dreadful day, one of his brothers, who also worked at the factory, had great difficulty in stopping Ted from cutting his own throat with a shoemaker's knife. The same brother had hidden all the razors and knives in the house because he was so frightened of what Ted might do to himself.

Ted's workmates noticed that he did very little work on Friday 26th July, but just stood around saying how ill he felt. On the morning of Saturday 27th July, before he left the factory to go home to Mary, Ted sharpened his knife and said that he was going to mend his children's boots. He wrapped the knife in his green cap and pushed them in his pocket and went home to number 76.

So if Ted Sewell was jealous, was he also insane? Suddenly what looked like a crime of passion might have a twist. But it was up to a jury to decide.

Sir Ryland Adkins, in addressing the twelve men assembled for the most serious task of their lives, reminded them that a prisoner was presumed to be sane until he was proved to be insane. He said it was not for him, representing the Crown, to prove Ted Sewell was sane, but for his learned friend, representing the prisoner, to prove that Ted Sewell was insane.

It had been an extremely violent crime from which the accused had made no attempt to escape. Was it the act of a man guilty of deliberate murder? Was it the act of a man yielding to jealousy? Or was it the act of a man caught in a moment of insanity?

Ted had already made a number of startling statements in court. ' I know I did it. I done it about 7 o'clock. We were both lying on the bed and I went downstairs to get a knife, she was nearly asleep. She never called out. I went out and got drunk. I know I shall hang. It's all through her going to Bell's.'

The jury retired for just 45 minutes.

'Is the prisoner Isaac Edward Sewell guilty of intentionally killing Mary Jane Pursglove?'

'Yes.'

'If so, was he insane at the time he did so?'

'Yes.'

'It is the sentence of this court that the prisoner be detained in a lunatic asylum until His Majesty's pleasure be known.'

The weather couldn't have been more of a contrast. On the Saturday, the day she died, it was hot and sultry. Now, Wednesday, it was a dreadful day, with a leaden sky and drenching downpours of rain: a crowd of mostly women gathered at the graveside. Sarah Smith from number 79 sent a lovely wreath. There were plenty of tears from her work mates and neighbours as the Wesleyan Minister, Mr Anderson, conducted the short, simple ceremony.

It was a touching sight as Elizabeth and Gladys tried to keep their composure. The plain elm coffin was lowered into the grave and the rain fell heavily on the wooden lid. It almost blurred the brass plate bearing the short inscription:

MARY JANE PURSGLOVE
Died 27 July 1912
Aged 36 years

THE BUTCHER OF DYCHURCH LANE

———————— ❀ ————————

Northampton 1892

The Black Lion in Northampton's St Giles Street has been a popular pub for centuries. Like so many old inns it has changed its name to make it 'trendy' and it is now called the Wig and Pen. The back wall of the pub is shared with the back wall of a building in Dychurch Lane that was once a butcher's warehouse. People say that sometimes, if you stand at the back of the bar when all is quiet, you can hear the sound of a baby crying.

Annie Pritchard was nervous and flustered and she hated rushing. She had gone to the Arcade to buy a few things before her journey so, when she arrived at New Street Station, she had to ask directions for the Liverpool train because she wasn't sure where to go. Birmingham's main station was big and busy, but the porter was helpful and, once he had pointed her in the right direction she fought her way through the crowds to arrive at her platform. The ticket collector told her she was on the wrong one and redirected her to another platform. By now she was even more flustered and was in tears. Her bags were getting heavier by the minute and her shawl was slipping and just when she reached the correct platform, she saw the Liverpool train steaming away from the platform.

Poor Annie was beside herself; it would be a long wait for the next train. She felt lonely and dejected as she looked around at all the strangers rushing back and forth. She found a quiet corner and perched on a bench. As she sat there, she thought about her brothers and sisters back in the comfy Highgate Road home she had left in Sparkbrook. She wondered if, by now, they had found the letters she had propped up by the biscuit barrel. 'Good bye' letters. 'Should I not be able to return home before I leave England,' she had written, 'I pray we may some day meet in a united family above. Wherever I am, be assured of this, I shall always be thinking of you and praying for you.'

Annie was the eldest in the family. She had three brothers and two sisters and had cared for them all since the death of their mother, and now they had grown and didn't need her. Her three brothers worked in the bicycle factory and brought in enough money to support the others. It had been a traumatic time for the family; they had lost their mother, father and young brother all within in a couple of years. In fact, they were still wearing mourning attire and, it seemed, had been doing so for far too long.

'I am sure I have quite fulfilled the promise I made to my dear mother,' Annie had written, 'to look after you younger ones till you are able to take care of yourselves, and on looking back on you, my dearest sisters – and Arthur – what little mites you were. What joys and sorrows we have shared.'

After giving so much time and care to her mother and her siblings, Annie was now free to lead her own life. Here she was on the threshold of an adventure and, although she had no idea what the future held, she knew that happiness awaited her.

At last it was time for her train and Annie started on what was to be the most thrilling journey of her life. When she finally reached Liverpool she was feeling unwell. The strain had taken its toll, but she was cheered when she saw that her beloved was there to meet her. He had met the train she had missed and had rightly presumed that she would be on the next one from Birmingham. Annie looked at him lovingly and thought how little he had changed. He, on the other hand, joked that he fancied she had altered a great deal.

Annie's next letter to her brothers and sisters, posted in Liverpool on 28th March 1892, must have been a huge shock to them.

'Well,' she wrote, 'I am no longer Annie Pritchard. We were married this morning by special licence and we are going to New York till my husband has completed his engagements, which will be no longer than six months, and then we hope to settle in England and be near you all. I hope that you will not consider my husband is too uppish to be introduced to you all. I am in much better spirits and I am looking forward to our return. I know I shall have a good husband in my dear Guy.'

Annie had told all her family and friends about her lover, Guy Anderson, although none of them had ever met him. She finished her letter by advising her sister Lizzy not to stay at home too much but to go and see 'Mrs Mac' as often as she could.

Now, Mrs Mac was the affectionate name Annie and her family had given to Mrs MacRae who had, until recently, lived next door. She and her husband, Andrew, had been married for twelve years and had two sons of eight and ten. Mrs Mac was caretaker at a local factory and Andrew had for some time worked for a glass manufacturer in Balsall Heath until it went out of business and then he had found alternative work. Fortunately his brother Edward heard about this and offered him a position ; the wage would be 30 shillings a week, and the job would entail working in Edward's meat warehouse and on a stall at Northampton market. It was a perfect situation and solved more problems

Dychurch Lane, Northampton, as it looks today.

than anyone could have imagined. Andrew's only regret was that he had to leave behind his horse and cart.

He took lodgings at 33 St John's Street in Northampton while his wife stayed at home in Birmingham. He went back from time to time to see her and the boys. He was popular with friends and neighbours and people thought him kind, steady, genial and affectionate. Someone even went so far as to say that Andrew MacRae wouldn't hurt a fly.

One morning in July, Andrew crossed All Saints Square and cut through the alleyway opposite the church that brought him to College Street. There he went into the tiny shop belonging to Mrs Louise Bland. She bought and sold clothes and, in those times when money was short, she had a good and steady trade. Andrew walked in carrying a bundle of women's and baby's clothes. He told her a sad tale: he had recently become a proud father but his poor wife had, following the birth, been committed to a mental institution. Louise Bland commiserated with him and gave him some money for the items of linen. A few moments after Andrew MacRae had left her shop, Mrs Bland paused: 'how strange,' she thought, 'most new fathers come 'ere to buy baby clothes, not sell 'em.' But what of it? It was none of her business.

Now this is where the story of Annie Pritchard takes an extraordinary turn. Annie was a dreamer and a romantic and most the events of that day on New Street Station and her journey to Liverpool never actually happened. She had made it all up. The whole elaborate and highly detailed story about missing the train, the journey to Liverpool and feeling ill, getting married, the prospect of America, all of it was fabrication. But why? She was in love certainly, but not with a man called Guy Anderson, and she had no intention of going to America with him, or with anybody.

No, the man she was in love with was Andrew MacRae.

Annie had, indeed, been on New Street Station on that day, but she was not travelling up to Liverpool, she was, in fact, travelling down to Northampton to meet Andrew MacRae. When she arrived at Castle Station in Northampton, she had a stroke of luck, she met a man called James Felley and, while she was chatting to him, she discovered that he was about to travel to Liverpool to see his family. It was at that point that Annie conceived the idea of writing to her brothers and sisters telling them that she had married and was about to go to America with her new husband. The man, Felley, promised that he would post the letter on his arrival in Liverpool. It was lucky for Annie that he kept his promise.

Annie met up with Andrew MacRae and together they went to the lodgings he had taken in St John's Street. For some reason they had taken the lodgings under the name of Mr and Mrs Anderson. Annie gradually found her way around and became familiar with the shops. Being a gregarious young woman, she became quite friendly with neighbours and with people she saw regularly. Most of them were really kind and helpful; that is how it always is with young attractive women in her condition. For Annie was pregnant.

Annie and Andrew MacRae's child was born on 23rd June 1892 in their Northampton lodgings. The new family planned on moving to 68 Derby Road soon after the birth. Annie had mentioned this to a new friend, Mrs Elliot. Then on 20th July, Annie and Andrew bumped into Mrs Elliot as they were walking near All Saints' church and they got talking. Annie, she recalled later, hadn't a care in the world and Mrs Elliot, like all cooing matrons, loved babies and Annie had let her carry the MacRae infant as far as the George Hotel. She went on her way, and the little family went on theirs. She thought they doubled back and went in the direction of Dychurch Lane, but she couldn't be sure.

That was the last time anyone saw Annie and her baby alive.

On Sunday 7th August 1892, Charles Hadley was walking home to East Haddon along the Northampton to Rugby road close to Althorp Park railway station. Country odours are one thing, but suddenly the air was heavy with the most ghastly smell imaginable. For some reason Charles wanted to investigate. Most people would have fled as quickly as possible, but not Charles. He climbed the railway bank and, with his stick, poked around expecting to find some kind of dead animal. With his handkerchief firmly clasped to his nose, and keeping well at 'stick distance', he saw in the ditch something that looked like a sheep. It was whitish, but he wasn't sure because he hadn't looked too closely and he wasn't about to look any more. By now the combination of the stink and the hot August sun was enough for him so he plodded off home, wondering. When he got to East Haddon he passed the Red Lion and he saw some of his mates leaning on the wall in the hot sunshine having a drink. Charles couldn't resist telling them about his find.

Life in East Haddon on a hot Sunday afternoon in 1892 was hardly filled with excitement so, when Charles shared his tale, his friends thought a stroll to the railway bank would be a welcome break from the monotony of the quiet, holy day. What they discovered when Charles took them to the spot, would ensure that the village was far from quiet for months to come.

Four days later, the *Northampton Mercury* startled the county. Under the headlines, 'A Northamptonshire Mystery' and 'Butchered and Beheaded' the ghastly details unfolded. 'A fearful discovery was made on Sunday on the road not far from Althorp railway station, the headless and armless body of a woman, tied up in a sack, being found secreted in a ditch. The body was in a frightfully decomposed state; indeed, it was on account of the fearful stench arising from the ditch that led to the shocking discovery.'

Charles and his friends had, indeed, uncovered the result of a dreadful crime. But this was no Sunday afternoon entertainment for amateur sleuths, so one of the men had run to alert the professionals. Superintendent Alexander of Northampton Borough Police arrived in due course. Later in court he said, 'I saw, lying near the ditch on the left-hand side of the road as you proceed to East Haddon, a bundle, which upon examination proved to be human remains.' He had poked the sack in which the body was wrapped and saw that the corpse was encrusted with lime. Two legs, like those of a rag doll, dangled and fell from the sack as the bag was split open. The body was fully dressed but the clothes were stained with blood. He looked around the ditch to see if the head and arms were lying near, but no. Superintendent Alexander found a local surgeon, Dr Churchouse, who happened to be in the village visiting. He examined the body where it lay. Then the torso was carefully carried, on a wooden pallet, back to the Red Lion that would, for the next few days, become both mortuary and courtroom.

An inquest was held in the pub the next day, Monday, and adjourned, and, in the days and weeks following, investigations took the police from that quiet village to Birmingham, London and many other places besides.

So what was known so far? There was a torso and some sacking. Not a lot to go on. The woman had been dead for over three weeks; that much Dr Churchouse had deduced. It was estimated that she was about 5 ft 5 ins tall; she was wearing a chemise, a nightdress, a pair of drawers, a pair of stockings, an underskirt and a good quality green skirt. Her lime-encrusted body was wrapped in a sugar bag and then in a rough sack. All this was clear but there was no indication of who she was, or of how she came to be in that ditch.

But then came the first real clue. On closer examination, one of the policemen noticed that on the outer sack was a luggage label. In the centre were the handwritten words,

'E. M. RAE. NORTHAMPTON', and printed in the bottom left-hand corner, 'L and N W R'.

E M Rae was not a common name. The 'Rae' part was especially unusual and it should be easy enough to track down. 'L and N W R' clearly indicated the 'London and North Western Railway.' The police wasted no time in tracing the origin of the label and the sack, and in locating the addressee. A London company called Warren and Sons supplied bacon and cheese to butchers and grocers and there was only one firm in Northamptonshire that used them. However, the company was not called E M Rae, but E MacRae.

Edward MacRae lived in Crick, a few miles north of East Haddon. He had a shop in the High Street in Daventry, a stall on Northampton market and a warehouse in nearby Dychurch Lane. Only a couple of months ago he had engaged someone to help him in his Northampton warehouse and on the market stall. That assistant was his brother, Andrew MacRae.

The inquest at the Red Lion pub resumed later in August. Both Edward and Andrew MacRae were called to give evidence. Andrew told the inquest that dozens of sacks containing meat were sold every month; anyone could have used one to conceal the body. It looked to the police as though the sack and the label, important as they seemed, would not help much in their enquiries. Superintendent Alexander still had no idea who the woman was nor who had left her beside the roadside.

Back on Tuesday, 26th July, Andrew MacRae suddenly regretted leaving his horse and cart in Birmingham three months earlier. He needed it here, now. Never mind, it would cost only a little to hire one. It was nothing like his own, this was just a simple dog-cart, but it would serve his purpose. On his way back from collecting the dog-cart, Andrew called in on Councillor John Banks who was a plasterer by trade and had premises in Abington Street. From him, Andrew bought a bushel of lime. Then, early on the morning of Wednesday, 27th July, before the sun was up, Andrew and his wife Annie took their last journey together. But the baby was left behind – somewhere – but no one heard him crying, at least not then. Andrew headed his dog-cart out on the Harlestone Road and drove towards East Haddon, stopping at Althorp Park railway station.

On Saturday 3rd September 1892, Andrew George MacRae was arrested and formally charged with the murder of an unknown woman. On the following Monday he appeared before the local magistrates and was remanded for five days. Meanwhile Superintendent Alexander and his investigating team had been very busy indeed. They had learned from their colleagues in Birmingham, that a young woman of 32, named Annie Pritchard, had left home six months earlier and, to the concern of her family, had not contacted them since. They thought she had gone to America with her husband, Guy Anderson, and that was all they knew but thought it strange that so loving a sister had not been in touch. Oddly enough though, a chance remark by Miss Lizzie Pritchard, sister of Annie, made the police stop in their tracks. Until quite recently, the Pritchards had been friendly with their next-door neighbours. They had moved away though, to another part of Birmingham, which was sad, because Lizzie had liked 'Mrs Mac'. Further questioning revealed that Annie had been rather friendly, perhaps more than friendly, with the husband of 'Mrs. Mac', Andrew MacRae.

In November, Andrew MacRae was brought to trial in Northampton before Mr Justice Kennedy. Nearly 50 witnesses were called and, throughout the case, Andrew never wavered from his plea of innocence.

Later in the autumn of 1892, the *London Star* newspaper carried a passionate plea. 'Let us have the truth if possible, and not kill a man before he is tried.' The plea was written by Mrs MacRae. So-called 'trial by the media' is something well known in the 21st century, but back in 1892 it was rare. As far as Mrs MacRae was concerned, there was absolutely no reason why her faithful and loving husband Andrew would, or could, commit so terrible a murder. At the same time, the court in Northampton was hearing ample evidence that was to prove otherwise.

It was not only Northampton's newspapers that devoted pages and pages each day to this crime, but also leading papers in London, Birmingham and elsewhere reported every gory and sensational aspect of the case that came to be known as 'The Haddon Horror'.

Eventually, on 24th December, after a five-day trial, Mr Justice Kennedy gave his summing up: it took five hours and was very detailed. He took pains to remind the jury of several points. The woman's torso was so decomposed that it was not really possible to say with any degree of authority how long it had been in the ditch. The identity of the woman relied only on the fact that Lizzie, Annie's sister, claimed under oath that she had seen Annie making the green skirt that was on the corpse. The judge did stress though, that Andrew MacRae had been publicly associated with Annie Pritchard in Northampton for some six months. Many witnesses had given evidence to that fact and many had confirmed that Annie had, on 23rd June, given birth to a baby boy at 33 St John's Street. It had also been confirmed that neither Annie nor the child had been seen for some weeks.

The jury retired for an 1½ hours. They came back to the packed and silent courtroom. Judge Kennedy asked for their verdict and in a clear voice, the foreman of the jury confirmed that they found Andrew George MacRae guilty of murder.

Pandemonium broke out. The judge had to call his courtroom to order. Edward MacRae was ordered to leave the court after he had shouted his brother's innocence. The crowd inside and outside the court broke into cheers. But Mr Kennedy was a patient and fair judge and, once order was restored, he asked Andrew MacRae if he had anything to say. The short speech he made must have moved those in the courtroom and those who read his words in all the papers later.

'Gentlemen, you have this day, each and every one of you, become what you have made me - a murderer. You have this day widowed a good devoted wife; you have this day, this night, Christmas Eve, made fatherless loving children. Go home to your homes. Can you with a clear conscience? Have you in giving your verdict, tempered your duty with mercy? I say no. As long as you live, your conscience will accuse you.'

But the words, emotional as they might have been, cut no ice.

It was assumed by one and all that Andrew MacRae had known that Annie was pregnant. So in order to protect her from scandal, and him from his erstwhile faithful and loving wife, he encouraged Annie to come to Northampton for her confinement. This was all right in theory, but MacRae soon realised that his 30 shilling wage from his brother, was nowhere near enough to support his wife and family as well as his mistress and their son. There was only one way out.

On Monday, 9th January 1893, Mrs MacRae received a final letter from her husband. In it he tried to convince her, once again, of his innocence. 'The jury,' he claimed, 'went into the box prejudiced towards me, with their minds made up as to the verdict. They took no notice,' he went on, 'of the learned judge, who was decidedly in my favour, and would, if left to him, have acquitted me.' He admitted to seeing Annie Pritchard in Northampton, but claimed that she had never been to the Dychurch Lane warehouse. 'Indeed,' he said, 'she had left Northampton Castle station at

8.35 that same evening for London where she was to meet Guy Anderson.' He went on to explain that Annie had written to him the next day telling him not to send her things on, but to sell them to help pay a few bills she had left outstanding. All his associations with Annie were innocent and kindly meant. In fact he was merely helping their old friend and neighbour out of kindness.

He was a creative liar, but did 'Mrs. Mac' believe him? Had she protested his innocence out of hopeless love or genuine faith in him? Certainly the liberal local paper in Northampton had a great deal of sympathy for her. In a leader column, the editor championed the cause of the abolition of the death penalty in a lengthy and erudite way. But it was, of course, too late. The black cap had been donned and the prisoner sent from 'this place'. Andrew George MacRae was hanged in Northampton Gaol on Tuesday, 10th January 1893. His body was removed from its original burial place due to development of the site. It was re-interred in Towcester Road cemetery.

Annie Pritchard's desolate family had already lost father, mother, brother and now a beloved sister. John Pritchard, Annie's remaining brother, had written to the *Northampton Mercury* on 10th September 1892, soon after the inquest at the Red Lion in East Haddon. In his letter he had thanked the residents of East Haddon and the Reverend Thomas Ruston for all their kindness and respect at Annie's funeral.

'It is a comfort to us all in the midst of our great trouble to think so much interest and respect should be shown by everyone to the remains of one, they knew not who. Had it been one of their own dear friends or relatives it would have been impossible to have paid the last tribute of respect in a more heartfelt manner.'

Annie's body, being the dismembered victim of murder, was not welcome in the local graveyards in that part of

Northamptonshire, but after the intervention of the Reverend Thomas Ruston, she was finally laid to rest in East Haddon cemetery. The headstone on her grave bears the inscription, 'I was a stranger and you took me in.'

No charge was ever made for the murder of a one month-old baby.

Andrew MacRae was hanged for the murder of an unknown woman. Her identity has never officially been confirmed.

THE THISTLES, THE RING
AND THE DEATH OF
A QUEEN

———————— ❁ ————————

Fotheringhay Castle 1587

The river, in this part of the county, takes on a different name. Down beyond Oundle and Thrapston they pronounce it Nen to rhyme with hen. North of Oundle, up here, it's Neen to rhyme with green. They look at you funny if you call it the Nen here. You are immediately branded a foreigner!

'Old-age rivers', as our geography master used to call them at school, the ones that carve wide curves in the gently undulating landscape, they don't flow as much as meander. Rivers like this have witnessed all sorts of things: ancient pioneers discovering new lands; merchants plying their trade; children swimming. Glimpses of every kind of event from life, and death – for rivers also witness death. Soldiers fighting battles, accidental drownings and murder!

The River Nene is no exception. From Naseby, where it rises close to the famous Civil War battlefield, through Northampton, where it saw Thomas Becket's trial, it gather's the county's stories into its arms, embracing key moments in the heritage of Northamptonshire.

And there can be few episodes more charged with emotion than the events of February 1587 when, up there on that mound, a young queen lost her head.

On 16 May 1568, Mary Stuart, the rightful Queen of the Scots, left the land she had ruled until her forced abdication, and set sail for England. For almost twenty years she would be a refugee, an itinerant, an alien but, most of all, she would be a prisoner.

She came to England freely and of her own volition, with the sole purpose of asking her cousin, Queen Elizabeth I, to help her. Mary could prove that she was the rightful heir to the throne of England, but she made clear that she had no intention of usurping Elizabeth. She was happy to wait, and if and when the Queen of England died, she could unite England and Scotland under her Catholic rule.

But help was not forthcoming and within a year, Mary was imprisoned. For nineteen years Mary was held captive by Elizabeth as trumped up charges against her ebbed and flowed like the tide. From the castles at Sheffield, Tutbury

The remains of the mound and court of Fotheringhay Castle. The fencing encloses the only stone remains.

and Wingfield, Mary kept her patience until finally she came to Northamptonshire – to the forbidding and solid fortress of Fotheringhay Castle.

She arrived on 25th September 1586, by now certain in her heart that her end was near. Her case was weak and everything and everyone had deserted her. All, that is, except God, for Mary did everything in the name of her staunch Catholic faith. If she could not reign on this earth as a monarch, then she knew that it would be her joy to die as a martyr.

Fotheringhay Castle had once been a royal residence; indeed, Richard III was born there. But now it was bleak and forbidding. Mary was very ill. All sorts of complaints and diseases wracked her body, but most of all rheumatism. Cold, damp castles made that worse. 'I cannot walk without assistance nor use my arms, and I spend most of my time confined to bed by sickness', Mary wrote. 'My advancing age and bodily weakness both prevent me from wishing to resume the reins of government. I have perhaps only two or three days to live in this world, and I do not aspire to any public position.'

Few of the rooms in Fotheringhay were furnished and Mary realised that she was virtually the only occupant, apart from her guards. It was becoming clear that she was about to meet her final ordeal. Before long, officials arrived from London and made hasty preparations for Mary's trial. A trial? How could this be? Mary could not be tried legally, she was a monarch in her own right, she was not subject to English law; she should not be tried by anyone. The only solution would be for her to be repatriated to her own country. But the trial went ahead. Her pleading was pointless.

'I am myself a Queen, the daughter of a King, a stranger, and the true Kinswoman of the Queen of England. I came to England on my cousin's promise of assistance against my enemies and rebel subjects and was at once imprisoned ... As an absolute Queen, I cannot submit to orders, nor can I submit to the laws of the land without injury to myself, the King my son, and all other sovereign princes. For myself I do not recognize the laws of England nor do I know or understand them as I have often asserted. I am alone without counsel, or anyone to speak on my behalf. My papers and notes have been taken from me, so that I am destitute of all aid, taken at a disadvantage.'

In those anxious years since leaving Scotland, Mary had held some keepsakes close to her heart, her rosary, Bible, and book of prayers. She had, of course, been allowed to keep and wear her jewellery, the rings with the huge precious stones and the one thing that she had kept to remind her of her marriage to Henry Stuart, Lord Darnley, the signet ring he had given to his beloved Queen on their marriage in July 1565. In addition to all of these, Mary had kept hidden in a silken pouch a handful of seeds that she had collected in her beloved Scottish hills. The seeds were thistles.

If you look carefully at the banks of the River Nene at Fotheringhay, the fields beside the water are thick with weeds. It is easy to dismiss them without a second glance, but these are no ordinary weeds. Look again. On the river-bank and up the side of the hill with its ancient gnarled hawthorns, there are thousands of thistles. These are *Onopordon acanthium*, the Scottish thistle. They are easily recognised and distinguished from the common thistle for these thistles have larger, more bulbous heads with longer spines. The stems are stouter and the leaves are tougher with long, sharp prickles. This is not a plant to argue with! This particular thistle is now common in eastern England, and it is said that it was here, in this lonely and mysterious spot, that it first took root. They are known locally as 'Queen Mary's Tears'.

In the few hours that she was allowed fresh air and exercise, Mary, supported by Jane Kennedy, Elizabeth Curle and her other faithful servants, limped along on the banks of the River Nene as her little Skye terrier ran ahead. This was a foreign country to her, and how better to give the flat landscape at least one hint of Scottish familiarity, than to cast some of those precious seeds that she had held so dear.

Ever since then, the Scottish thistle has grown in profusion, bearing witness to the presence, albeit unwilling, of a queen in her last days on this earth.

Following her trial, in which everything she said was dismissed, Mary languished in Fotheringhay Castle from the middle of October 1586 until February 1587. Then came what her guards saw as a sign from heaven. On the Feast of St Paul, 25th January, there was an incredible thunder storm. Lightning more violent than any that had ever been seen, tore across the sky and turned the darkness of Mary's midnight cell to daylight. Three times it crashed and three times it blinded her guards, who later recounted the event with breathless fear. Mary was convinced that she was to face death and waited patiently for the warrant of execution from Elizabeth. When finally the document arrived and was read to her, she sighed with relief, 'I thank you for such welcome news. You will do me great good in withdrawing me from this world out of which I am very glad to go.'

That evening, Mary chose to be alone in her room. She made copious notes on who should have her valued possessions. Some were to go to her royal relations, others to her faithful servants, but one ring would not be given to anyone. Its fate would be yet another mystery in the events of Mary's imprisonment at Fotheringhay. It was the betrothal ring that Henry Darnley had given to Mary before their marriage on Sunday 29th July 1565. Was it on that night, the night before she died, that she decided to rid herself of the ring forever? Did she stand at her window and look below to the clouds of Scottish thistledown? And did she decide there and then to add the ring to that small fiction of Scotland that she had created? Whatever happened that night, Mary was not in possession of that ring at nine o'clock the next morning. For that was the time she was taken, dressed all in black velvet, to the great hall where some 300 onlookers had assembled to witness her execution.

There was one man present at the execution who was dissatisfied with the evidence against Mary. He was one of the commissioners appointed by Elizabeth I, but he did not want the Scottish queen's blood on his hands. He was Edward, 11th Baron Zouche of Harringworth in Northamptonshire, not a dozen miles from Fotheringhay. He was from the same family as Hugh Zouche, the subject of another mystery elsewhere in this book. But Edward Zouche's objections were over-ruled and by 10 am it was all over. It was Wednesday 8th February 1587 and Mary Stuart, Queen of the Scots, as a result of an illegal trial, had been murdered at the hands of a cousin she had never met.

In 1820, long before the days of metal detectors, Robert Wyatt was merrily rummaging through the rubble beside the River Nene. He found something amazing and he couldn't believe his eyes. He was a romantic, and for years he had found fame locally for showing people round what little was left of Fotheringhay Castle. The site was then much as it is today: a huge mound covered in hawthorn and thistle. The hawthorn seeded by passing birds. The thistles, the Scottish thistle, descendants of the precious seed cast by the woeful Mary over 200 years before.

At that time, the castle site was part of Castle Farm and, already in ruins, was used for grazing. No one thought the castle of any importance, it was simply a good and convenient source of building material. Many houses in the village used stone from the ruins, as did buildings in nearby Oundle, including the famous Talbot Hotel. The fact that Richard III was born in the castle in 1452 and that Mary was executed there a 152 years later seemed to mean very little.

But Robert Wyatt was different. To him, the place

The Darnley Ring. (V&A Images, Victoria and Albert Museum)

breathed history, mystery and romance. The farmer, with Robert's help, had filled in a bit of the moat here, and dug out a bit of stone there and had carted off the foundations of the drawbridge. In the process, odd artefacts were dug up; early coins from Edward II and IV and so on, but what were old coins after all?

It was while Robert was alone one day on the castle mound, kicking around in the soil and gravel, that he saw something metallic, but dull. He bent over and picked it up. It looked like a ring. He gave the ring a bit of spit and polish (he had been a soldier), and studied it more closely. It was a signet ring bearing a lovers' knot bound up with the monogram 'MH'. Inside the ring was an inscription. Robert

Wyatt could hardly believe his eyes, it said 'Henri L. Darnley 1565' with a lion on a crowned shield. Robert held his breath. Could this be the signet ring that Henry Stuart, Lord Darnley had given to his beloved Queen Mary on their marriage in July 1565? The marriage proved to be a great mistake, but that aside, here was he, Robert Wyatt in 1820, holding the token of that union in his work-hardened hand.

The ring was given to experts who studied, verified and accepted it as, indeed, Mary's ring. Robert was given a subscription for his find and he died in 1862, a happy man.

And the ring? It is now part of a collection of betrothal rings housed in the Victoria and Albert Museum in London. Over the past 20 years, some experts have doubted the ring's authenticity, but Richard Edgecumbe, the V & A's Keeper of the collection doubts their doubts! One of the experts who first saw the ring in 1820 wrote, 'Perhaps it dropped from Mary's finger in her death agony on the block, and was swept away among the bloody sawdust, unobserved'.

I like to think she threw it from her window on her last night on this earth.

THE BLACK WATCH AT LYVEDON

Brigstock 1743

On a green mound in Northamptonshire sits the ghost of a soldier shrouded in a long, dark mantle, and if you listen on the breeze, you might even hear the sound of phantom bagpipes. The ghostly figure is a member of the great Royal Highland Regiment, the Black Watch, and for one brief moment, the history of the Regiment and that of Northamptonshire came together.

Northamptonshire has had strong connections with Scotland for centuries. In 1328 the Treaty of Northampton that gave Scotland its independence; in 1587, Mary, Queen of Scots was executed at Fotheringhay (as noted in the previous chapter); and in the 1930s, Corby received a huge influx of steel workers from Clydeside. Along with them, they brought many customs from north of the border and second-generation Corby citizens even have a unique accent that is something between Northamptonshire and Lanarkshire!

So a story about the Black Watch may not seem all that unusual, but this is a story that is not recorded in the official history of the Regiment, for it tells of mutiny, desertion and murder.

The countryside is wide and open on the road from Brigstock to Oundle. Two miles due east of Brigstock, where

Lady Wood, near Lyvedon New Bield. (Trevor Rhodes)

the shallow hills rise gently up to the tree line, is Lady Wood. It is right on the edge of the ancient Rockingham Forest, favourite hunting ground of Norman kings. It is hereabouts that you might find the low green mound that locals call 'The Soldier's Grave'. There was a time when superstitious country folk would never go there after dark and certainly never on or around 22nd May, for that is when the ghost of a solitary soldier of the Black Watch can be heard piping and, some say, can be seen sitting, shrouded, on the mound.

Like most folk tales, this one is firmly based on fact. Tradition has it that the grave is that of a soldier of the Black Watch who died, or was killed, in Lady Wood in 1743, a key date in the Regiment's history.

In the 1740s, relations between England and Scotland were fragile and it was rumoured that England could be invaded by the Scots. These fears were, of course, realised in 1745 with the Jacobite Rebellion. In 1743, the newly formed Royal Highland Regiment, that came to be known as the Black Watch, was ordered to march to London to join the British Army. The soldiers thought they were to be inspected by George II, but they found on their arrival that the king had gone away into Germany. They encamped at Finchley, and time hung heavy and stories and rumours abounded. One rumour in particular gained ground and caused alarm and, eventually, tragedy. Word spread that the regiment was to be sent to the West Indies, which, in those days was known as 'the white man's grave'.

Eventually, the king returned to London and, being advised that the Black Watch was awaiting His Majesty's pleasure, he summoned two members of the regiment, Corporal McPherson and one other, to St James's Palace. After the audience, the two soldiers were given a guinea each. The proud Scots regarded this as an insult and as the news of it spread amongst the ranks, disquiet began to rumble until, on 17th May 1743, 136 soldiers of the Black

Watch deserted. They took arms and ammunition and stole away during the night, headed north and set out for Scotland.

They travelled mostly under the cloak of darkness and so progress was slow. They slept in barns on the way and begged for food and drink. They managed to get as far as Northamptonshire, and contemporary reports say that they were first seen in Wellingborough. By 22nd May they had reached Lady Wood, near Brigstock, where they sought cover in the trees. But then their escape was foiled. Word of their desertion had clearly preceded them and the local militia had been alerted. The brave, but exhausted soldiers were surrounded and forced to surrender their arms, but not without a skirmish.

Thirty-six soldiers escaped (and were caught elsewhere), but 99 were taken prisoner in Lady Wood that day. The hundredth man never left the place alive, he was buried beneath Soldier's Mound. How he died, we will never know. All the soldiers were taken back to the Tower of London and were tried by court martial. Most were disciplined and then absorbed into other regiments. Corporal McPherson and two others were shot and were buried where they fell.

It was a tragedy that should never have happened. A glorious and brave Regiment had been misled and manipulated, and honest soldiers had been forced to do something completely out of character. One solitary soldier remains in Northamptonshire, buried beneath the green grassy mound of Soldier's Grave in Lady Wood. If you listen as the breeze rustles the leaves on the trees, you might even hear the pipes playing the lament.

THE CHARWELTON MURDER

---❂---

Charwelton 1821

Good people all of each degree,
Give ear unto my tragedy,
Which I am going to unfold,
It is as true as e'er was told.

During the period of King George IV's reign, the prurient could satisfy their morbid interest by reading amazingly full and detailed accounts of scandalous trials in newspapers. If it had a strangely compulsive 'folk' appeal, they could read it in verse on a broadsheet. If the trial had been particularly celebrated, and the case especially bloodthirsty, enterprising publishers released the details of the whole case in pamphlet form. One such noted publishing house was Dicey and Smithson of Northampton and eight pence would have secured a thrilling best seller.

In 1821, Dicey's published 'The Trial of Philip Haynes and Mary Clarke for the Wilful Murder of John Clarke, late of Cherwell House, in the Parish of Charwelton on the 10th Day of February last.'

It was a case that immediately caught the imagination of the public. It was all about infidelity, adultery, jealousy, violence and, of course, murder. It was a winner!

At Charwelton Northamptonshire,
A wealthy farmer lived there,
One Mr Clarke he had a wife,
But lived a most unhappy life.

Charwelton is a pretty village today, full of the glorious golden ironstone dwellings that are peculiar to Northamptonshire. One of the most fascinating features is the magnificent 13th century packhorse bridge that once carried merchants and footpads, old dreamers and young lovers over the River Cherwell. Once it leaves Northamptonshire's borders, the River Cherwell babbles on through the north Oxfordshire countryside until it reaches Oxford. There it flows into the famous River Isis, scene of picnics in summer and students punting. Once it leaves Oxford though, the Isis is called the Thames. So, by deviously tracing it back, we can almost say that the Thames rises in Northamptonshire!

In Charwelton the river is, in truth, little more than a trickling stream as it runs under the bridge, for it is still a young river. It's source was at one time in the cellar of Cherwell House, but the old farmhouse has been demolished. It was the house where John Clarke lived – and died.

John Clarke was a well-to-do farmer and a pillar of local society. He had a lot of land round his farmhouse on the edge of the village, half a mile from Hellidon, and so for him money was not a problem. He had lived a fairly solitary life though and longed to share it with someone, so he took a mistress. Her name was Mary and she was 35 years old, almost half the age of 67-year-old John. Naturally, she was something of a gold-digger; it was never thought that she was in love with John. But, she moved in and shared John's life and in the early days of their union, she did all that was expected of her and, of course, she helped on the farm.

But Mary had a secret. John Clarke had no idea that Mary had, for some considerable time, been having an affair with Phillip Haynes, a labourer from the next village of Byfield. Indeed, she had a child by him, but the babe had died after having been farmed out to a friend.

After a while, Mary realised that she had made a mistake; the arrangement was not working as she had hoped and there were rows and John was making too many demands on her. Money or no money, she left and took refuge in Northampton. It did not take John Clarke long to locate her and, with the carrot of a settled and lucrative marriage proposal on the end of a stick, he enticed her back. Mary and John married and, although they had two children, it was never wedded bliss. But Mary was still seeing Phillip Haynes. Indeed, so determined was she to include him in her life, that she convinced her husband into thinking that extra help was needed on the farm and she knew the very man!

Cherwell House, demolished in 1978.

Phillip Haynes, of course. John Clarke was not unhappy with Phillip's work, he was a good and conscientious worker, but it did not take him long to notice that Phillip was spending too much time with Mary rather than on his labouring duties. Phillip Haynes was sacked and he went back to Byfield, where he stayed with Mary's friends, Elizabeth and John Bush. John Bush would later tell the court that he had worked for Mr Clarke for 30 years and that Elizabeth had also been at Cherwell House right up to Clarke's death, 'She went there a good deal for nursing and other things'. In fact, she had 'nursed Mrs Clarke when she laid in of both her children'.

> *Then this unfortunate Phillip Haynes*
> *For carnal lust and curséd gains*
> *Soon yielded to her cruel will*
> *Her husband Mr Clarke to kill.*

In his evidence at the trial, Bush also told of two things that would take on great significance. He recalled that, about a year before his death, John Clarke was hurt by a fall from his horse and also that he, Bush, had received a parcel and letters from Mrs Clarke with the request that he deliver them to Phillip Haynes. The fall from the horse may not have held much significance at the time, after all, Clarke was a farmer and riding was his main means of getting round his farm. But the reason he fell from his mount was because a rope, tied between two trees in a spinney on his land, had caught him on the chest and had forced him to the ground. How was it that a rope should have been so positioned? And how interesting that it was actually on a route he used often when he returned from visiting friends. But how lucky that the rope hit him on the chest and not a foot higher, on his neck, for that would have killed him instantly.

Later that week, Elizabeth Bush was discussing John Clarke's accident with Phillip Haynes. 'I told Haynes that Mr Clarke said his horse had tumbled over some stones, but Haynes told me he had tied a string across the road, which had thrown the horse down. I said, it was a pity he had done so, Haynes said he did not mean to hurt him. Mrs Clarke knew of this. She said he was a very bad husband to her.'

And what of the parcel and letters sent from Mary to Phillip with Bush as the go-between? Had no one ever realised that they might have been more than just the orders of an employer's wife to a labourer? That they might, as was the case, have been intimate letters, love letters, plotting letters? Indeed, portions of these letters, over 50 of them, were read out in court as evidence, and they alone would have sealed Mary's fate as an accomplice to a heinous crime.

*'I could be happy if the Old ***** was dead.'*

'If it is not done in a short time, I cannot see what will be the end of it – I wish you would do it as soon as you possibly can.'

'You must have another plan. When the night grows dark you may hit on him, and get another pistol, which will carry. I pray day and night, it may be done between now and Christmas.'

'I wish you would send me some Laudum (sic) and I will see what I can do for him – I will do it if I can – send me that or something else.'

'I pray you to do all you can to get shut of him, for there is nobody knows what I go through, but God and myself. But do him, do him if you can.'

Not the sort of thing you read in innocent letters between mistress and employee.

It was obvious that for some time Mary and Phillip had been meticulously planning John Clarke's death. In fact, three attempts had been made on his life. The incident with the rope in the spinney had been a bungled attempt and had caused a dreadful argument between Mary and Phillip. The next was equally amateur: Phillip had made a cosh and he had hidden behind a gate and, like a cartoon burglar, had leapt out and hit Clarke on the head causing little more damage than double vision! The third try involved laudanum, but this time it was Mary who failed by giving too weak a dose and rendering her husband merely to complain of sickness.

The secret lovers were now even more resolute. The prize was huge. Mary would inherit the farm and Clarke's wealth. She would rid herself of an old fogy whom she hated, she would be able to live in bliss with her handsome lover and he, incidentally of course, would do very well out it the crime too. 'You must have another plan – get another pistol', another plan, another pistol? This was serious, Mary insisted that Phillip buy a pistol and do the job properly. With considerable persuasion, he went to Brackley and bought a horse pistol and all the requirements. Everything was set to do murder.

> *To scheming then they did proceed,*
> *The safest place to do the deed,*
> *Says Haynes, I'll go into the barn*
> *For there no one can me discern.*

Phillip Haynes hid himself in the barn and, in amongst the barley, he assembled a veritable hoard of essential supplies. The gun, his wallet, a wooden bottle, a glass bottle, some bread and bacon, a powder flask, a small thick-twilled

THE

TRIAL

OF

PHILIP HAYNES

AND

MARY CLARKE,

WHO WERE TRIED AT THE LENT ASSIZES FOR THE

County of Northampton,

On the 8th of MARCH, 1821,

Before the Honourable Sir JOHN RICHARDSON, Knight,

One of the Justices of our Lord the King, of his Court of Common Pleas;

THE FORMER FOR

THE WILFUL MURDER

OF

JOHN CLARKE, late of Charwell House,

IN THE PARISH OF CHARWELTON,

In the said County,

FARMER,

On the 10th Day of February last,

And the latter (who was the Widow of the said JOHN-CLARKE), as an ACCESSARY to the said Murder before the Fact:

TOGETHER

With their subsequent

CONFESSION.

NORTHAMPTON:

PRINTED AND PUBLISHED BY DICEY AND SMITHSON; AND MAY BE HAD OF THE BOOKSELLERS IN GENERAL; AND OF THE NEWSMEN CARRYING THE NORTHAMPTON MERCURY.

PRICE EIGHT PENCE.

1821.

[ENTERED AT STATIONERS' HALL.]

The title page of Dicey's 'best selling' account of the trial.

cotton bag containing lead and shots. At about 3.30 on the afternoon of Saturday 8th February 1821, Phillip Haynes fired the shot. It caused a serious injury to his victim's left arm, serious enough to confine Clarke to bed, serious enough to call for the doctor, serious enough for Clarke to want to settle his affairs.

Robert Wildgoose was the surgeon from Daventry who was called to attend Clarke on that Saturday afternoon. He arrived at about 6 pm and found the patient exhausted from loss of blood. The principal wound was in the under part of the elbow joint and there was another wound higher up. 'The first wound was so large,' he said in court, 'that I could put my fingers in. The amputation took place at 9 pm that night, we had waited,' he went on, 'until Mr Clarke had made his will.'

Finally, it appeared, John Clarke realised the gravity of the whole murderous business. Another John Clarke, a local magistrate, took the instructions of the will. 'I thought it better that he (the dying man) should not know that Haynes was in custody until he had signed the deposition,' the magistrate said in his evidence, 'when signed, I told him Haynes had been taken and on expressing his wish to see him, I ordered Haynes into the bed-chamber. Haynes came to the foot of the bed and asked, with great concern how he did. John Clarke looked at him and with his remaining hand pointing towards him, said, 'You bloody minded fellow, how could you do me this unkind office?"

Investigations revealed that Haynes had, indeed, hidden in the barn and it was from there that the shot was fired. During the search, Haynes was discovered, hiding in the barley. Some farm workers were prodding the barley with their pitchforks when one of the farm workers, Anthony Marriott, trod on someone's foot. A voice said, 'Be civil and I will get up', it was Haynes. Marriott said, 'You rascal, I have a good mind to stab you – you did not mind killing my master.'

Phillip Haynes, still denying the shooting, was taken into custody. John Clarke died early the next morning. It was now a case of murder.

> *At the Assizes they were brought*
> *To answer for their cruel fault,*
> *The jury soon did guilty cry*
> *And they were both condemned to die.*

A week later, Mary Clarke was arrested and was accused with being an accessory before the fact in the said murder. The lovers were tried before Sir John Richardson at the Lent Assizes in Northampton on 8th March 1821. The jury, after a short consultation, returned a verdict of guilty against both the prisoners.

Phillip Haynes and Mary Clarke were hanged on 10th March 1821.

> *Now let their fate a warning be,*
> *To all of high or low degree,*
> *Be constant to your bosom friends,*
> *Then God will bless you to the end.*

THE BONFIRE NIGHT BLAZE MURDER

Hardingstone, Northampton 6 November 1930

Remember, remember, the fifth of November …

If you know where to look you can still find the grave, and if you happen to meet one of the older villagers, they'll take you to it. You have to go around the church and then you'll see it quickly if your eyes are sharp. It's covered in ivy now, and the grass in the churchyard gets long and untidy, but there it is, a simple wooden cross with the chilling inscription, 'In memory of an unknown man. Died Nov 6 1930'. It's a pleasant final resting place, under the old trees and close to the golden stone walls of the 13th century church tower. And luckily, it's well away from that road; the one where it all happened.

Lillian gave Alf his overnight case that he'd packed himself as he always did. He said 'Goobye' and left. Lil had no idea that when she saw him again it would be in very different circumstances. She thought she was living in a nightmare already, in a loveless, pointless sham of a marriage. But that was nothing to what was to come.

Alf's car was a shining black Morris Minor 'Baby', his pride and joy, and as good as new. It really was his 'baby' and he kept it in marvellous condition. He had a string of 'babies' of a different kind, but that's another story. As he drove down Buxted Road fireworks were going off all round. He always remembered bonfire night from his youth, and perhaps this one would stick in his mind too, but for a different reason.

Fireworks were all right, but he didn't like the 'bangers'. They disturbed him, they reminded him of the shellfire in the war and the head wound he got in 1915 at Festubert in France, the wound that had such a strange effect on him ever since.

He left Finchley just after 8 pm and headed for the North Circular so that he could get on to the road for Northampton and then Leicester. On his way he did two things: first he stopped at a garage and filled a gallon can with petrol, and then he stopped again and picked up a hitch-hiker. It was a regular run and Alf knew the route well; he worked as a 'rep' for a Leicester firm that made garters and suspenders. Garters and suspenders! It couldn't have been a more appropriate line of business and if it sounds a little sleazy and distasteful, even better, for that was the kind of life Rouse led. That head wound had changed his personality and his relationships, he was now a serial predator with a propensity for seducing women wherever he went. Four score reported cases of seduction were to be laid before him later and countless charges of paternity.

Rouse was not a wealthy man. He earned £500 a year but he'd bought several cars over the years, the latest was his new Morris Minor 'Baby' and he was paying £1.12s a week for that. The house cost £750 and there were payments of £1. 7s 6d on that too. And then there was the 10 shillings a week in maintenance that he had to pay Helen Campbell for the child; one of his unfortunate liaisons that had caught up with him and had gone through the courts! Oddly enough, Helen had met Lil and it was agreed that the boy should live in the Rouse home. It was an extraordinary set-up.

Alf Rouse.

There were others too. Like Nellie Tucker, he paid her 12s 6d a week for his two children – when he remembered. And Ivy Jenkins: Rouse had gone as far as actually marrying her, and one or two others. And he had women in Birmingham, Southampton, all over the country in fact. But clearly, with all these dues to meet, and leading so many double lives, by 1930 he was pretty desperate and all he wanted was a way out of his financial and marital problems. He longed to make a fresh start, but how?

He had read with interest an article in the *Evening Standard* back in January 1929 and it kept flashing across his mind. He was always fascinated by stories of espionage and crime: this one combined both and it intrigued him. It was all about a man in Germany who had killed a passenger in his car so that he could get the insurance money. He had forgotten all the detail, but it's funny how bits of stories gently 'simmer' away on the back burner of your mind and then bubble to a fast boil later.

But this was 1930 and Rouse was hoping to disappear without trace. In actual fact he was about to be the star attraction in one of the most famous cases in British legal history.

The usual Thursday night dance had been brought forward to the Wednesday night in order to celebrate Guy Fawkes' Night. William Bailey and Alfred Brown were cousins and they had been to the dance and were on their way home up the London Road to Hardingstone. It was a very bright moon-lit night and as they turned into Hardingstone Lane they saw, a short distance ahead of them, a bare-headed man climbing through a hedge and on to the road. And then, as they looked over the hedge through which the man had emerged, they saw the glow of something burning. 'What's the blaze?', Bailey asked his cousin. The answer to his question came, not from his cousin, but from the stranger who, noticeably breathless, said, 'It looks as if some one has had a bonfire'.

The cousins continued towards the fire. The stranger by now had reached the main road and was dithering over which way to go. Then he stopped and watched Bailey and Williams and realised they were hurrying now, because clearly what burned before them was no ordinary bonfire. When the two cousins had that chance encounter, it was the worst thing that could have happened to the man they met. For he was Alfred Arthur Rouse and it was he who had started the fire that was, at that moment, consuming the body of a completely unknown man. It was now just after midnight on 6th November 1930.

As Bailey and Williams neared the blaze they saw that it was a car, so they ran off to Hardingstone and to Bailey's father, who was the local village bobby. Together with another constable, they all ran back to the fire. As the flames began to subside a little, they could make out a human head and bits of a body in the car. They called for a more senior policeman, Inspector Lawrence, who took copious notes at the scene, but failed to have any photographs taken at the time. By four in the morning the charred and mutilated corpse was taken, wrapped in sacking, to the garage of a pub in Hardingstone for security until it could be delivered to the General Hospital in Northampton later that morning.

At this stage, the police had not thought the incident was in any way connected with 'foul play'. They treated the incident as little more than an unfortunate accident. A photographer was allowed to take pictures of the burnt-out car and in aiming for a better 'shot', he moved what was later to be seen as crucial evidence. The police cleared the charred remains of the car and piled them on the grass verge, assuming that there would be an insurance enquiry and an inquest. The one thing they clearly did not suspect was murder. What they did do, as a routine, was to issue a statement saying they were anxious to contact a man aged between 30 and 35, 5ft 10ins tall, with a small, round face and curly black hair, wearing a light mackintosh, dark trousers, no hat and carrying an attaché case. It was in all the papers the next day, including a picture of the car. Then the police, using information relating to the car number, MU 1468, called at the house in Buxted Road where Lil was requested to go to Northampton to help with enquiries. Although they would not let her see the body, she was reported as saying that the braces, buckles and bits of clothing could have been Alf's.

Alf Rouse abandoned his plan to 'disappear off the face of the earth', and decided instead to hitch a lift in a lorry back to London. He called at his home, without disturbing Lil and from there went, by bus, to Cardiff and then to Penbryn. That was where Ivy Jenkins lived, the woman who called herself Mrs Ivy Rouse, the one Alf bigamously married five months earlier, the one who was carrying his child!

Things then start to move very quickly. Next morning, Alf read in the *Daily Sketch* an account of a burnt-out car in Northampton, together with a rather disturbing description of a man named as Alfred Arthur Rouse! The Jenkins's had seen the paper but Alf denied the story and asked Ivy's friend to drive him to the coach station so that he could go to London. But the friend grew suspicious because of things Alf said on the short journey. The man talked to a local journalist who alerted the police, and the police were there to meet Alf on his arrival at Hammersmith Bridge coach station at 9.20 on 7th November.

Did Alf make excuses? Did he weave yet another of his improbable tales? No. His first words to the awaiting plain-clothes policemen were, 'Very well; I'm glad it's all over. I was going to Scotland Yard about it. I am responsible. I am very glad its over. I have had no sleep.' Arguably, the most truthful words Alf Rouse had spoken for years. He was taken to the police station and later transferred to Northampton police station which, in those days, was in

Angel Lane. He made the most amazing confession. In it he claimed that he had picked up a hitch-hiker near St Albans and, when they arrived at Hardingstone, he said he was drowsy, the car was spluttering and he wanted to go for a pee. The passenger asked him for a cigarette. Rouse had noticed that his passenger had his hand on Rouse's attaché case so, when he stopped the car, he took his attaché case and told the passenger that there was a spare can of petrol in the boot, and would he put it in the petrol tank while he went off to relieve himself. Then, while he was some distance away, he saw the car on fire. He did his trousers up and ran to the car, saw the man inside, tried to open the door but couldn't because of the heat. After a while, he climbed through the hedge to get help and saw two men.

Convincing or what? Unfortunately, Rouse was all talk. He had wooed all his women with his smooth tongue and they believed every silken word he'd said. How would he fare with the police? Unfortunately, he went on to say just a bit too much. Having woven this wonderful story, he then started to get personal. He started to go on about how Lil was too good for him. How he was going to sell up and separate from Lil. How he had a harem and it was expensive. Why did he use the word 'harem'! The papers, of course, loved it. Later in court it was disputed whether or not the impression given by the papers had been prejudicial to the case. The press had certainly had a field-day in describing every sordid aspect of his life.

Rouse's insurance company confirmed that from 18th July 1930, his policy had been increased, giving a healthy £1,000 pay-out, should there be a death of a passenger in the car. But who was the passenger in the car? That is the one fact that was never determined. The police were satisfied that there was a case to answer. Rouse appeared before the magistrates in November and December 1930 and was sent for trial at the Northampton Winter Assizes on Monday

The cross in the churchyard at Hardingstone (Trevor Rhodes).

26th January 1931 before Mr Justice Talbot. Counsel for the Crown was later to become one of the stars of the English legal process, Norman Birkett, KC MP. Did Rouse's Counsel, Douglas Finnemore stand a chance? The red-bound copy of the trial report contains 316 pages of small print and amazing photographs. Expert witnesses were called and recalled. References to other cases were made. The jury was asked to leave during repeated discussions over intricate matters of law. Evidence was deemed admissible and then inadmissible. The public gallery heaved with excitement. Below them stood a very handsome, lithe and vulnerable man who was sexy and virile; the women liked that! He was 'a bit of a lad', a philanderer, a man with a few dark secrets; the men liked that! And of course, the press loved every minute. But the fact that Rouse was a bigamist, a cad, a liar and rotter were incidental to the matter in hand. Was he a murderer? It may have been written up as a wonderful case for law students to study because of its intricacy, but in purely human terms, it is a story of a man who, for a variety of reasons, found himself drowning in a sea of troubles, and went the wrong way in his attempts to resolve them. Of course he was a murderer, and it took the jury just 15 minutes to return their verdict. Rouse paid for his crime at Bedford prison at 8 am on Tuesday, 10th March 1931.

Remember that article in the *Evening Standard* of January 1929? The one that kept flashing across Rouse's mind? The one about a man in Germany who had killed a passenger in his car so that he could get the insurance money? In fact it was all about a man called Karl Erich Telzner. It seems that he confessed eventually and, two months after Rouse died on the gallows, Telzner paid for his crime at Regensburg on 2nd May 1931.

Nice to have all the ends tied up. All, that is, except, who is buried under the wooden cross in Hardingstone churchyard?

THE GHOST AND THE UNPAID BILLS

❁

Barby 1851

I can hardly remember a time when I didn't know about the Barby ghost; I suppose it was something I grew up with. As a lad, during the holidays, I used to cycle from my home in Daventry over to Barby to spend the day with my friend John Powell. Sometimes I would stay the night and cycle home the next day. It was a wonderful adventure, exploring the village with John on our old Raleigh bikes, but the best part was investigating his house. His father was the Rector of Barby and the house in which the family of three lived was huge. Built in 1869, it was Victorian Gothic at its most elaborate, with pointy window frames, a huge porch and doors and staircases everywhere. The red brick was decorated with big yellow diamond patterns all over the outside walls (I now know that it is called diapering). But my lasting childhood memory is of the many lavatories the rectory had. I think there were seven. We had two in our house and we thought that was grand! The rectory was demolished years ago and the whole place is buried beneath houses.

I don't recall who first told us about the Barby ghost. Perhaps it was the old odd-job man who cut the grass in the orchard at the rectory, and who used to fill our minds with

Widow Webb's cottage in Barby (Barby Historical Society).

all sorts of country wisdom. I didn't know all the detail of the story then; that came only when I called in on some of the older villagers about 25 years ago, and they simply couldn't wait to pass the tale on to me. One of them had read the story in an old hand-written book that was found in the rectory. I hope the story is still told to a new generation in Barby.

Widow Webb died in her bed at two o'clock in the morning on 3rd March 1851. The sad thing was that nobody really cared. Even the two people closest to her – her neighbours Mrs Griffin and Mrs Holding – were probably relieved. They had cared for her over the past month during her illness, but they had received little thanks for their efforts. They could carry on with their own lives now that she'd gone.

Barby, near Daventry, was like most villages. Everybody knew everybody else, and everybody pretended not to interfere in anyone else's business, even though, in truth, everyone was nosey and loved to pry! So when Widow Webb died, the gossips of Barby really did have something to talk about. Widow Webb was a tall, slim woman of 67. Late in her life she had married William Webb, a tailor who had done very well for himself. When he died, he left a lot of money; in fact it was a small fortune for those days. Of course, all the money went to his widow. They lived in the centre of a row of thatched cottages with neat gardens in front and a shared path leading up from the road. Next door to the cottages was Brackenfield House. It was a large and quite imposing farmhouse that stood well back from the road. It belonged to Widow Webb's nephew, Job Hart. He was a miller and farmer.

At the beginning of February, Widow Webb had become ill and had relied on Mrs Griffin and Mrs Holding, who lived either side of her. Sadly, Widow Webb was something of a miser and gave her neighbours nothing for all their care. Nothing, that is, but trouble both in life and in death. Widow Webb's money along with the cottage was left to Job Hart. Shortly after Widow Webb was laid to rest in the churchyard at St Mary's, Mrs Griffin and Mrs Holding mistakenly thought they had seen and heard the last of the miserable old woman. How wrong they were. Often, during the night, they began to hear dreadful banging and clattering noises coming from the Webb cottage. Since the cottage was now empty the noises seemed to be magnified. The two ladies were troubled by the noises but there was little they could do apart from mention the matter to Job Hart. He told them that their worries would soon be at an end for, in April, they would be glad to hear, the cottage was to be let to a Mr and Mrs Accleton and their ten-year-old daughter. Mrs Griffin and Mrs Holding couldn't have been more delighted. A family moving in, at last they would have a nice new set of neighbours.

The Accletons moved in, met their neighbours, Mrs Griffin and Mrs Holding, and looked forward to a pleasant new life in the village. But very soon, strange things began to happen. A few weeks after they had moved in, the Accleton child awoke screaming at 2 am. She claimed that she had seen a tall, slim woman standing beside her bed shaking her head. The girl's mother dismissed this as a childish nightmare. The move had unsettled her, she was not used to the new surroundings. Mrs Accleton found all sorts of reasons for the nocturnal disturbance. She calmed her daughter, waited with her until she fell asleep and then returned to her own bed. But then the same thing happened at 4 am and again, seven times over the next seven nights. Mrs Accleton did not see the tall woman in the beginning, but later, with Mrs Holding, Mrs Griffin and another neighbour Mrs Radbourne, she did see the apparition. The four women had huddled together, in the dark, terrified. The appearance of the ghost was accompanied by streams of light shining around a trap door in the ceiling, though at the time, they thought little of this.

News of the ghostly goings-on spread round the village and reached the ears of the curate, the Reverend John Carey, and the rector the Reverend Charles Williams. Normally the clergy would have regarded such things with suspicion but the two Barby clerics listened eagerly to the events from the Accleton cottage. The rector considered an exorcism, but on reflection he decided that might be a little dramatic. Being something of a local historian, Mr Williams simply wrote the story down for posterity!

Mrs Accleton complained to her landlord, Job Hart. She related the story in all its terrifying detail, later remembering to tell him about the way the light had centred on the trap door in the ceiling. Job Hart, a man not given to such supernatural happenings, agreed that the two of them should investigate the trap door, and, to his amazement, in a corner of the roof-space, Job Hart found some papers and a bag containing gold coins and bank notes.

It was William Webb's fortune. Job Hart claimed the booty and left. For a while, Mrs Accleton thought perhaps their nights would no longer be disturbed. But within a few days the banging and crashing continued. Then by chance, back in Brackenfield House, Job was looking through the papers he had found and spotted some unpaid bills. Being a good businessman, he paid the bills using the cash from the attic. From that moment on the noises stopped. The ghost never appeared again and everybody, including Widow Webb rested in peace.

THE VALLEY OF DEATH
AND LORD CARDIGAN

❖

Deene Park, near Corby

Although he is remembered as a great national hero, the Earl of Cardigan seemed to go hand in hand with death and violence throughout his 71 notorious years. So it is no surprise that he is forever associated with Tennyson's 'valley of death'. After a lifetime of controversy – military, political and personal – Cardigan met his end, as he would have wished, on his beloved horse, at his beloved home.

Deene Park has been home to the Brudenells since 1514. And James Thomas Brudenell was, without doubt, the most celebrated member of the family for in 1837 he inherited the title that would be carved into English history. He was the 7th Earl of Cardigan and his name would be inextricable from the Battle of Balaclava and that most unfortunate incident, the Charge of the Light Brigade.

Cardigan loved to live dangerously. He took incredible risks in the hunting field; at one point he was thrown from his mount and nearly drowned in the River Welland because he could not swim. He was sexually adventurous too, cited by many aristocrats for dalliance with their wives. Indeed he had an affair for two years with a married woman before her divorce enabled her to become his first wife. He was forever having duels and earned the reputation of 'The Homicidal

Lord Cardigan, Sir Edmund Boehm's plaster model for the marble monument in St Peter's church, Deene.

Earl'. Following one duel in which he injured his opponent, he was arrested for an act of felony and the case went to the House of Lords. It was the first time in 46 years that a peer of the realm had been tried for a felony and it caused a sensation. Eventually, the 120 peers unanimously found him not guilty.

Most of all, he was a soldier through and through, 'I always had an inclination for the service from early youth' he once said, and when, as the 22-year-old Lord Brudenell, he joined the Northamptonshire Yeomanry, his dream became a reality. Then at 26 he joined the 8th Hussars, managing to combine this with being Member of Parliament for Marlborough. He lost the seat at Marlborough, but gained a seat in Northamptonshire. Then, when he was 44, his violent and masochistic streak came out in its full colours. Cardigan had few friends and many enemies, a natural result of his arrogance, his predatory nature and his love of the chase, whatever the quarry. One famous and inhuman incident on Easter Day in 1841 nearly lost him his reputation for ever.

Cardigan was a disciplinarian and, in the army of the day, flogging was the discipline that would, most of all, bring the men into line. It was a ritual that nowadays would be condemned with the utmost severity, but in 1841, it was actually enjoyed by those with the twisted sense of right and wrong that obtained in Her Majesties Army. It was not uncommon for a man to be strapped to a frame in front of his regiment, and given anything from 25 to over 1,000 lashes by the victim's own fellow soldiers. By the time Cardigan was in command, the number of lashes had been restricted to 100.

On Easter Day, of all days, Cardigan had ordered a man to be flogged. The combination of the flogging, the perpetrator, Cardigan, and the most holy of days in the Christian calendar raised public opinion to boiling point. The unpopular and despised peer was now hated and the press fanned that flame of hatred with relish. 'When will the public have done with Lord Cardigan?' was the cry from *The Globe*. The matter was raised in the Commons; the

Church intervened; the Government condemned the act but Cardigan survived and remained in command of his regiment. The bloodthirsty Earl was left to go on to further acts of foolish triumphalism.

Thirteen years later came the Crimean War. The ins and outs of the Battle of Balaclava and the suicidal Charge of the Light Brigade have been well documented. It was all a matter of misunderstanding and bungled orders, but Cardigan, even though he knew the orders would spell disaster, remained arrogant to the last and would and could never admit culpability. Here was death on a massive scale. Only 195 mounted men out of 675 survived. In one section, only 14 men were counted back out of the 150 who charged, and 475 horses perished. Death and Lord Cardigan had come dangerously close again. But he survived once more and came home a hero. He was fêted by the Emperor of France and celebrated by Queen Victoria. The poet Laureate, Lord Tennyson, immortalised him and his disastrous charge in the poem that every loyal Victorian child learned by heart. Cardigan was even to be promoted to Inspector of Cavalry.

He returned to Northamptonshire where he was given a hero's welcome in the county town. The bells of All Saints and St Giles churches rang out for him, flags flew and, as his carriage left St John's station and drove up Bridge Street to the town centre, a band played Handel's 'See the conquering hero comes'. One and a half centuries later it all seems like hollow acclaim.

Back at Deene, he set about making sure that his brutal exploits were never to be forgotten. He commissioned artists to capture him and his great successes in paint, bronze and silver. Vast paintings that still hang at Deene show the Charge and other bloody frays as vividly as a 'still' from a war film.

But death was finally to catch up with the erstwhile indestructible Earl. It was said by his opponents, that the sight of a corpse engendered an irresistible fascination in Cardigan. On 26th March 1868, he was riding with his second wife, Adeline, when a member of his staff rode up to say that one of the gamekeepers had been killed when a gun accidentally exploded. Cardigan, of course, rode off in great haste eager to see what had happened. A little later, having comforted the dead gamekeeper's sister, Cardigan rode back towards Deene and exchanged a few words with an estate worker on the way. A moment or two later, the worker heard a cry and then saw a child running towards him. The child, in a panic shouted that a man had fallen off his horse. Sure enough, Cardigan was lying on the ground, his face blue and heavily bruised, foam was issuing from his mouth and his head doubled beneath him. Ronald, the Earl's trusted charger, that had seen him through every great campaign including Balaclava and the Charge, was standing pathetically by.

Lord Cardigan died two days later without speaking another word. Lady Cardigan, like her late husband, also had a strange fascination with death. She gave the Earl the most remarkable funeral at Deene with Ronald walking immediately behind the coffin. After lying in state for two days in the ballroom at Deene, Cardigan's body was brought to the small church of St Peter on the estate, where it was entombed. The monument to him continues the theme of controversy that followed him throughout his life. On top is a monumental sculpture to Cardigan and to his second wife, Adeline. The two are lying side by side, gazing lovingly at each other. He is in the traditional pose of a military nobleman. She is lying beside him in a strangely seductive way, with her peeress's robes loosely draped around her. The monument was designed by Sir Edgar Boehm, Sculptor in Ordinary to Queen Victoria, and one of the greatest artists of the Victorian age. It was one of his early commissions, created in 1869, within a year of Lord Cardigan's death.

Lord Cardigan's charger, Ronald, preserved in a glass case at Deene.
Ronald went on to live for another 18 years after Balaclava and
outlived his master by four.

Adeline, Lady Cardigan, the grieving widow, posed for
Boehm and dictated exactly how she should appear in
marble. Then she gave a banquet on the occasion of the

unveiling of the double monument. The sculpture of her, in repose and joined in death with her husband, was unveiled 46 years *before* she died! Life for her was just about to begin.

She too led a scandalous life and she was not too long in widow's weeds. In August 1873, after twelve proposals of marriage from a variety of titled suitors, she married the Portuguese nobleman, Don Antonio Manuelo, Count de Lancastre, and brought him back to Deene. On her many jaunts around Europe, Adeline antagonised Queen Victoria by styling herself not Lady Cardigan, but the Countess of Lancastre, a title dangerously close to one that Her Majesty used when she travelled incognito, the Countess of Lancaster. Following his death in 1898, Adeline remained at Deene and grew more eccentric by the day. She was often to be seen on a bicycle, bare-legged riding round her estate, dressed in her husband's uniform or a kilt and with a blonde wig atop a gaudily painted face. Most bizarre of all, she used to invite guests to dinner, disappear to change clothes, and then have her guests summoned to the ballroom where Adeline had placed the coffin that she had ordered from Oundle in readiness for her demise. As the guests filed in eager with curiosity, they beheld Adeline, in a white silk dress and the ubiquitous blonde wig, lying motionless in her coffin.

Today, the only truly macabre features of Deene are contained in a glass cabinet in the Great Hall. They are the head and tail of Cardigan's horse Ronald who outlived his master by four years. On the morning of Cardigan's funeral, Ronald had to be sedated with laudanum and as a result, he had to be roused by a bugler who sounded the 'Charge'. Ronald, out of habit, rallied into action. It was a touching moment as the faithful horse that had seen so much death, led his master to his final resting place.

THE BOXING DAY MURDER

---❁---

Northampton 1868

> *Roast beef and marsh mallows*
> *Says the bells of All Hallow's.*
> *Roast beef and boiled*
> *Says the bells of St Giles'.*
> *Pokers and tongs*
> *Says the bells of St. John's.*
> *Shovel, tongs and poker*
> *Says the bells of St Pulchre's.*

The very thought of a Victorian Christmas conjures up a picture of smiling faces, traditional fare, carols, peace and harmony. But for two families in Northampton in 1868, it was to be a time that would change them forever.

James Kemp and his wife had moved from Birmingham to Northampton with their two children. He was a wonderful father and a hard worker. They were a happy family, looking forward to a quiet, but festive time in their small home. Nearby, in the same part of Northampton, lived the Bridgewater family. The father, John, was a widower with a grown-up family. His sons, Edwin, Henry and William would be gathering with him for a few days over the Christmas season.

The church of the Holy Sepulchre is the oldest building in Northampton and is the oldest, largest and best preserved of the four surviving 'round churches' in England. It dominated

Campbell Square. PC Kemp was murdered very near here (Reproduced by permission of Northamptonshire Libraries and Information Service).

the area in which the Kemps and the Bridgewaters lived. In the old rhyme it was called St Pulchre's, but is familiarly known as St Sep's. The Crusader Round that stands at the heart of the church dates from 1100 AD and was built as a thank-offering by the first Norman Earl of Northampton, Simon de Senlis, on his safe return from the First Crusade. In the 19th century, the area around St Sep's was a close and vibrant community. There is nothing left of that community now, except the church and a few fine Georgian houses further down on Sheep Street and Barrack Road. Most of the working people lived in or around Campbell Square in terraced cottages on Victoria Street, Lady's Lane, Newland and other streets that have disappeared forever under car parks or civic buildings and shopping malls.

John Bridgewater's son, William, was brought up in that part of Northampton, known as the Mounts. In 1868, at the age of 38, he was married with a family, but he was parted from his wife. They had lived up on the Mounts, but William had been lodging in Wellingborough. He had worked as a shoemaker for some time and had become a skilled machinist and he had, in fact, actually been the inventor of two or three machines for the industry and as such he could really have made something of his life. But William Bridgewater had a serious problem. Like many working men in the late 1860s, he liked to go for a drink after work. In his case, though, one or two drinks had a personality-changing effect on him. He ceased to be the industrious, skilled family man and became monstrous, unpredictable, irresponsible and very dangerous. His wife, unable to handle his behaviour, had left him, and his children lived in fear.

On Thursday 24th December 1868, Christmas Eve, William Bridgewater and his fourteen-year-old son Alf, travelled by train to Northampton's St John's station with the intention of spending Christmas with William's father at 34 Victoria Street, off Campbell Square, a matter of yards from St. Sep's churchyard. John Bridgewater had a large family. As well as William, he had two other sons, Edwin who kept the Plumber's Arms in nearby Sheep Street, and Henry, a shoemaker who lived and worked in Leicester. There were also daughters living at home. Henry had come down from Leicester for the Christmas holiday. The family exchanged news, helped prepare and serve the meal and then sat down for supper on Christmas Eve. William told the family that he was going out shooting on Christmas Day; he liked to boast that he was well-known in all sorts of places, including Althorp Park, and that he had only to mention his name and he would be admitted to a shoot.

After supper, William left the house and went to Edwin's pub where he intended to sleep for the night since there was little room at Victoria Street. This he did and the next morning, he caught the train back to Wellingborough. Whether or not he went shooting on Christmas Day we don't know but, on Boxing Day, he went to call on a friend,

Thomas Allebone, in Wellingborough, to borrow a double-barrelled shotgun, telling his friend that he was going shooting small birds with his brother. He caught the train back to Northampton and went directly to the King William the Fourth pub that still stands at the bottom of Bridge Street. There he met up with another friend, Charles Robertson. William had clearly been drinking and when he and Robertson left the pub and walked up Bridge Street towards to town centre, William began picking an argument with some men who had gathered on All Saints' Square.

Robertson managed to get William away from the potential flash-point, and together they passed the magnificent portico of All Saints and went up The Drapery into Sheep Street. William had said that he wanted to leave his gun with his brother Edwin at the Plumber's Arms. Edwin was not in the bar when they arrived and so the gun was left with a girl who put it behind the bar. William told her some tale about there having been some trouble in the street. Someone bought William a glass of ale, but he drank only half of it. He had a disagreement with another customer over absolutely nothing, and slapped him on the face. William left 15 minutes later, and said he was going to his father's house. This he did and asked his father about his son, Alf. He took the lad away for a while and then Alf came back without his father, who had returned to his brother's pub. By now it was about 10.20 pm. William had been drinking but, by all accounts, was not incapably drunk. He asked for the gun. Edwin's wife, Lucy, gave it to him and told Edwin that William had taken the gun. She also told him that William appeared excited and that it caused her some concern.

Edwin knew how excitable William could be when he had been drinking, but he also knew other things about William's past behaviour. He knew that he suffered from deep depression and that four years ago, while he was working in the shoe industry in Staffordshire, he had attempted suicide by hanging himself. He had also tried to cut his wrists, and had tried to poison himself, and had threatened to poison the whole household. He had also held a pistol at his mother and his son. William was clearly not to be trusted, especially if he had been drinking and even more so, if he had a gun. Edwin felt that he must warn his father and the rest of the family in Victoria Street. So he left for the family home.

Meanwhile, William called in at Charlotte Harris's beer shop in Newland. It was the first time Mrs Harris had ever seen William. 'You don't know me, do you?' he said to her and she said she didn't. He told her his name and that he had been out shooting all day in Althorp Park. Mrs Harris looked at the gun. 'You're timid about this gun, aren't you?' William said. 'I am', she replied, 'is it charged?' He told her it was, but that it was not capped. Later, when recalling his visit to her beer shop, Mrs Harris confirmed that, in her judgement, William was perfectly sober. He left Mrs Harris's shop and went to his father's house in Victoria Street, just three minutes walk away. He knocked loudly. Normally he would simply have walked in, but for some reason he stayed on the pavement and banged on the door. Henry answered the door and was surprised to see William standing there. William, who still appeared to be quite sober, shouted, 'Send Alf out'. Henry told William to come in, 'I won't' he shouted, 'I want Alf, and will have him'. William's father, John, tried to persuade William to leave the boy in his care, but William insisted and off he went, dragging Alf who was in tears.

After two minutes, young Alf returned, saying that his father had boxed his ears and sent him back. Edwin arrived 10 minutes later to warn his father that all was not well with William. The father's response was to bolt the door firmly. Then, almost immediately, there was a knock at the door. John Bridgewater shouted, 'Who's there?' It was William, but the door remained locked. William shouted that he had come back for Alf, but his request was refused, John Bridgewater said that it was too late to let the boy out. William shouted and ranted and was clearly agitated. Henry meanwhile, went to an upstairs window and saw William on the pavement and, in the half-light, he could see that his brother had a gun. Shouting from the upper window, Henry asked what he wanted and said he would call the police if William didn't go away, to which William said if he did he would shoot him. Henry challenged this and said he daren't shoot. Again William said, 'If you holler 'Police', I'll shoot.' Henry thought his brother was joking, so he leaned out of the window and shouted 'Police!' at the top of his voice. At this, William backed into the middle of the street, aimed the gun at the window and fired. Fortunately the shot missed Henry and hit the bedroom ceiling.

Henry ran to the police station in Fish Street, five minutes away, but as he left, he heard the click of the hammer on the gun; Henry was in range of William, but the gun did not go off. Once summoned, Inspector Beattie of the Borough Police set off immediately with a couple of officers.

It was a dark and cold night. In the area around Campbell Square there were scores of pubs and drinking establishments, so there were revellers on the streets continuing their Christmas celebrations. William had followed Henry across Campbell Square, towards the town centre. Just then Samuel Wills, George Crisp and James Kemp were walking round the corner of Newland and along Lower Mounts towards the Square. James Kemp was a policeman. He was dark haired with dark whiskers, rather florid and with a round face. Sam Wills pointed to William Bridgewater and remarked to Kemp that he looked drunk. Kemp went forward to see what he was about and William said, 'Don't follow me.' Kemp was about ten yards away, when William lifted the gun and fired. He had shot Kemp, hitting him in the neck. Kemp cried, 'I am shot, I am shot, that man has shot me.' William Bridgewater, the gun still in his hands, ran towards Upper Mounts and on to Victoria Street. There were a great many witnesses to the shooting, groups of locals going home, passers by and residents who ran from their homes around Campbell Square. Many were shouting 'Murder! Murder!' One passer by, William Dunkley, approached the panicking fugitive. 'The next bastard that comes near me,' William Bridgewater cried, 'shall have the next fire.' James Kemp began staggering after his assailant. He grabbed the coat collar of his friend Sam Wills and then collapsed on the pavement. William was running towards his father's house in Victoria Street with Wills following him. By which time, two policemen had taken hold of William, and his father had forced the gun out of his hands. William was crying like a baby, 'I know I shall be hung for it; it will be the death of me and my poor old dad.'

James Kemp was taken to the infirmary where he managed to give evidence of the shooting to Charles Wickens, Clerk to the Magistrates. 'I am one of the borough police-constables,' he said, 'and left duty a little after ten and went up Newland to Campbell Square and there I saw a man. He had something in his hand. I have looked at William Bridgewater and think he is the man. He said, 'Keep away or I'll shoot you'. I thought he was joking, and I did not like to be a coward. He told me to keep back and then I saw a flash and felt I had been shot in the neck'. During that interview in the infirmary, William Bridgewater and James Kemp came face to face. 'Do you think I intended to hurt you?' William asked. 'I don't know', was James Kemp's reply.

When he arrived at the police station, William said, 'I'll give it to you straight, I did shoot him, and I meant to shoot somebody, I meant to shoot my brother. I am sorry I injured Kemp.' At the trial in Northampton, witness after witness confirmed that William Bridgewater had a chronic drink problem and that it caused him to become very excitable. No-one was able to confirm whether or not there had been a dispute between William and his brother Henry, or with any other member of the family, although it was mentioned on several occasions that William resented the fact that his father had refused to let him take his son, Alf, on that fateful night.

What was going through William Bridgewater's mind as he crossed Campbell Square that night? He had admitted that he was out to shoot somebody. Who? If it were his brother Henry, then why? Surely not his father for he had no reason to do so. No other enemy had emerged in the trial and there was never any suspicion that there was anyone with a vendetta against William. As he crossed the square, knowing that his brother had hailed the police, did he, in his drunken and agitated state, think that PC Kemp and his two friends were his brother and two policemen, instead of one policeman and two complete strangers? Whatever the reasoning, or lack of it, behind the crime, James Kemp was shot for no reason. It was unprovoked, pointless, cruel and mindless. James Kemp died in the infirmary on the morning of 29th December 1868.

The judge in summing up laid all the facts before the jury. The twelve men stayed out for just fifteen minutes before returning. Their verdict was that William Bridgewater was not guilty of wilful murder but guilty of manslaughter. Public opinion thought otherwise. It had been reported in the account of the coroner's court in January that, 'The jury said they were unanimous in finding a verdict of wilful murder against William Bridgewater.' Regardless of the outcome of the trial in the assize court, it was difficult to erase that first 'not guilty' verdict from the minds of the public.

The police have always held a very special position in society and the death of an officer whether on or off duty is something that could neither be accepted nor forgiven. The leader column in *The Northampton Mercury* 13th March 1869, rightly reflected the mood of the people. 'In this country there is little sympathy for murderers who select servants of the Crown as their victims,' it said, 'under these circumstances, we can hardly regard the sentence of Twenty Years' Penal Servitude as unduly severe'.

Appropriate it may be, but for many in the close-knit community around St Sep's in Northampton in 1869, it was not enough.

THE UNQUIET SOUL

---❀---

Rockingham 1415

Modern tourists come to the Welland Valley for a variety of reasons, for there is much to see. But two vast structures dominate the skyline. Harringworth Viaduct spans the valley, but Rockingham Castle commands it! The two buildings are separated by 812 years of amazing history, and the communities in which they stand are connected by a story of romance, mystery, tragedy and murder.

The great viaduct that crosses the River Welland is the largest in England. It was started in 1876 and took two years to complete. It is ³/₄ mile long and some 60 feet maximum height. There are 82 arches, each of a 40-foot span. Four hundred men helped by 120 horses built the viaduct using 20 million blue bricks made on site.

But Harringworth also has treasures of an earlier age including the church of St John the Baptist, parts of which date from before 1200, and the village cross that has stood at the heart of the community since 1387. There are also some important domestic buildings dating from medieval times, for Harringworth was once home to a family called La Zouche who first settled in here in 1150, when Alan la Zouche came with his wife, Princess Constance of Brittany. Since those early days, generations of the Zouche family have lived in the village and, indeed, in 1386 Sir William was given a licence by Richard II to enclose and fortify his house therefore creating Harringworth Castle, now known as the Old Manor House. Another branch of the family settled in Leicestershire and gave their name to Ashby de la Zouche. A later Lord Zouche was to sit in judgement over the unfortunate Mary, Queen of Scots at Fotheringhay.

Rockingham castle is a magnificent fortress proudly and defiantly overlooking the vast valley spread at its feet. Its strategic position was first appreciated when Iron-Age man built a fort there. Then the Romans and Saxons defended themselves from this breathtaking spot. The present castle was built in 1066 by order of William the Conqueror, and since then it has been a favourite of monarchs as a fortress and as a hunting lodge. It hosted important Councils of State and from it, great decrees were issued. King John was the most frequent of all royal visitors; he came regularly to hunt in the ancient Forest of Rockingham. As a Royal residence, it was kept fully staffed and was a hive of activity; in fact even to this day it is like a small village within the great castle walls. It took a great deal of maintenance in order to be ready for the times when the king decided to arrive with his court. The estate had to be managed and the vast Royal Forest of Rockingham had to be administered. Rockingham remained a royal castle for 553 years, until it was sold to the present owners, the Watson family, in 1619.

Hugh La Zouche lived and worked at Rockingham Castle as constable. He was born in nearby Harringworth in 1379. His parents, William, Second Baron la Zouche and Elizabeth, lived at Harringworth Manor and had six children: five boys and one girl. Hugh was the second youngest in the family. During the reign of Henry V, life at Rockingham was as busy as it had always been. The king first came to hunt there in 1413 as soon as he inherited the throne. He enjoyed the sport at a time when his somewhat reckless existence was, through royal duty, being forced into the serious and challenging role of kingship. Life at

Rockingham Castle (Reproduced by permission of Northamptonshire Libraries and Information Service).

Rockingham Castle had treated Hugh la Zouche well. He had a position of authority suitable to his station, he had influential friends at court and he had a beautiful wife who, with their son, lived with him in the castle. But the intrigues of castle life cast a deathly shadow over Hugh's life. Little did he know that his years of happiness would be replaced by years of torment and that, after his earthly presence in Rockingham Castle had ended, he would continue to haunt its battlements for centuries to come.

One day Hugh la Zouche was out hunting in the forest with his friend, Lord Neville. Something was on Neville's mind and eventually, when they took a break from the chase, Neville confided in his companion; he said that Hugh's wife, Alice, was being unfaithful to him. Hugh protested, claiming that he had never had any suspicions of infidelity on his wife's part. No, he simply couldn't believe it. But Neville insisted, saying that Alice was often to be seen in the castle in the company of a young squire. It was becoming the subject of gossip and he felt that Hugh should know from him, rather than from some less authoritative source. Naturally this news came as a terrible shock to Hugh. He was passionately in love with Alice, but now he was tormented and torn between his love for her and the consequences of her betrayal. Anger overtook him and he left Neville and rode back to the castle in search of the adulterous couple. At last his search ended. He found Alice in a remote part of the tower; she was standing close to a cloaked figure. Without a word, Hugh ran the stranger through with his sword and the body collapsed to the floor. Alice screamed and fell to her knees caressing the dying mystery man. Hugh threw his sword aside and pulled away the hood of the cloak to identify the demon who had robbed him of his beloved wife. To his horror he discovered that it was not a young squire at all. It was not even a man. The creature before him oozing blood was none other than his sister-in-law who had, tragically, disguised herself as a young man. She had fled the convent in which she had been forced to live by her parents and, with Alice's help, was seeking refuge at Rockingham in order to meet her own lover of whom her parents had so disapproved. Hugh was beside himself with remorse. He regretted his untypical outburst of anger, and was desperate for an explanation for this dreadful chain of events. He rode off into the forest to confront Neville, who had brought about this tragedy. It seemed like an inexplicable act of mischief. On his way, in the depths of the forest, Hugh had a strange vision. He saw the spectre of a friar who told him that all was lost and he must return to the castle. He was doomed to misery and his line would die out forever. Mystified and terrified by this, young Zouche immediately gave up his hunt for Neville and headed back to Rockingham Castle.

What awaited him was yet more tragic. Earlier in the day, Neville had followed him back to the castle and had hidden in the shadows where he had witnessed the dreadful murder. As soon as Hugh left for the forest on his search for his erstwhile friend, Neville had followed Alice to her apartments where her son was playing. There he brutally murdered Alice and the boy. He too left for the forest in pursuit of Hugh. On the very same spot where Hugh had had his vision, Neville too was intercepted by the ghostly friar. The sight of the phantom caused Neville's horse to rear up. Neville was thrown off and, as he fell, he received a fatal blow and landed face down in the River Welland.

Back in the castle, Hugh was heartbroken. He had no idea why all this had happened, let alone what Neville's reason might have been. It crossed his mind that maybe Neville had loved Alice and was jealous of Hugh. Whatever it was, it caused Hugh mental torture and for seven nights, he wandered the battlements and dark corners of the castle, punishing himself for the evil deed he had done. He went to the chapel and buried his head in his hands, weeping uncontrollably and praying for forgiveness. He remembered that the Apostle Peter had asked Our Lord how many times he should forgive a brother who wrongs him. The Lord had replied, 'Not seven times, but seventy times seven'. Hugh cried aloud and pleaded with God for forgiveness.

On the eighth day, Hugh died on the very spot where his sword had pierced that innocent heart. It was Holy Cross Day, 14th September 1415. Each year on Holy Cross Day, the ghost of young Hugh la Zouche walked those dark places until finally, in 1905, the ghost appeared no more. This was exactly 490 years later, seventy times seven. Perhaps his dreadful sin had been forgiven and the corridors of Rockingham Castle were finally at peace.

THE SYRESHAM MARTYR

John Kurde of Syresham, near Brackley 1557

*Take your seats for Syresham, for Syresham's the place
Where they never, never worry nor fall into disgrace.
Where all the boys are brothers and all the girls are sweet,
If you tumble down in Syresham, they'll set you on your feet.*

So runs the old village rhyme. But it was not always so, for poor John Kurde fell, and neither his loyal brothers nor his sweet sisters could save him and set him on his feet.

On the wall of the Wesleyan chapel in the village of Syresham near Brackley, is a memorial tablet to John Kurde who died in 1557. But his death was shrouded in hatred and superstition. It was carried out by men who were under orders from a woman. And they all believed that they were acting in the name of love. In modern parlance his death would be called murder, but in the bloody 16th century it was called justice.

John Kurde, like so many men in Northamptonshire, earned his living as a journeyman shoemaker. Shoemaking was Northamptonshire's most celebrated trade. The leather in the county was good and stout; all along the River Nene were great oaks and the bark from these provided the tannin for the tanning process. So the boots and shoes made here were the best you could get anywhere. King John is recorded as having bought his favourite boots from Northamptonshire.

Cromwell's army was supplied with boots from here and ever since, the county has been famous for supplying shoes to the world. The trade was as old as time and John Kurde had learned at his father's knee. He worked in a small barn in his yard and he would sit for hours at his bench and his lasts, clicking and skiving, stitching and closing, using the ancient methods that had been handed down for centuries. He travelled on foot from village to village picking up his business, often stopping for a few days and mending boots in an inn stable in the more distant communities, as well as spending time in Syresham to do the main body of his work.

But John Kurde was a man whose strength was not only physical, it was spiritual as well. His faith was the very essence of his life and it was to be the reason for his death. Like that other great Northamptonshire shoemaker and champion of the faith, William Carey, who lived almost 200 years later, John Kurde seemed to be just a simple tradesman, but in reality he was a man of great intelligence and fervent determination. It is hard for us in the 21st century to understand the religious climate of the mid-16th century, but religious intolerance had become part of the accepted pattern of life and it would continue for another century or so.

Henry VIII had created the great break with Rome. The Reformation that started in Europe had arrived in England, and an English Protestant Church was emerging. After Henry's death, his weakling son Edward VI was manipulated by his uncle, the Duke of Somerset, who did all in his power to move England fully towards Protestantism. In 1549 the First Prayer Book (the first ever in English) was published and that was the most significant change for the worshipping people of this country. Religious belief was ordered by Acts of Parliament. In fact the Prayer Book was an Act of Parliament and any deviation from it constituted an illegal action resulting in imprisonment and possible death. It sounds quite incredible to modern ears, but that was how things were then.

In 1551 a law was passed rejecting the Catholic doctrine of transubstantiation, the notion that in the Holy Communion service, the bread and the wine, after being blessed by the priest, become the actual body and blood of Jesus Christ. And for the first time, Articles of Religion were outlined in English. These formally rejected all Catholic teaching and put forward a new Protestant teaching in a form that allowed the 'man in the pew' to understand what was happening during divine service.

John Kurde was a fairly average 'man in the pew'. He loved his religion and, with the advent of a service in English, he embraced Protestantism wholeheartedly. Because of his occupation as a shoemaker, John Kurde travelled around the area, met people and discussed important matters with them. Ideas were exchanged. Significantly, Syresham, that small village in the heart of the Royal Forest of Whittlewood, was on the main road from Oxford – a seat of learning, radical thinking and reform. Kurde would almost certainly have been influenced by scholars who passed through on their way to Northampton and elsewhere.

Then came a period of extraordinary events in the royal household. Edward VI was not expected to live. The Duke of Northumberland, Edward's new controller, feared for the future of the Protestant church since the staunch Catholic, Mary Tudor was next in line. So Northumberland forced Edward to 'illegitimise' his two half-sisters, Mary and Elizabeth, so that the succession should go to his daughter-in-law, Lady Jane Grey, who was also the great-granddaughter of King Henry VII.

Edward VI died at the age of sixteen, Lady Jane Grey was proclaimed queen, and Mary Tudor's supporters persuaded the Privy Council to proclaim her as rightful heir. Lady Jane

Engraving of the execution of John Kurde (Northamptonshire Libraries and Information Service).

Grey, after only nine days, was taken to the tower and Mary became Queen.

England once more became a Catholic country.

It is important to remember that not all of England had been willing to embrace the new Protestant religion. In fact, even during Edward's short reign, the opposing factions had almost caused a civil war. So when Mary came to the throne public opinion, perhaps surprisingly, rested with her and she was, in spite of her cruel streak, popular. But her popularity was short-lived. She took her powers too far. She married Philip of Spain, but the English parliament refused to accept him as king, and Mary blamed the whole dreadful situation on Protestant heretics and she determined to rout them out. During her reign of terror, almost 300 Protestants were burned at the stake. No wonder she is remembered in history as Bloody Mary. Burning at the stake had been employed since the Council of Verona in 1184 when it was made the official execution for heretics. Successive Lateran Councils confirmed this and it was, therefore, accepted as part of Catholic doctrine. Joan of Arc was probably the most famous heretic to be burned at the stake and, in the opinion of the English, her only crime was witchcraft. The line between heresy and witchcraft was extremely thin in the eyes of fanatical medieval religious authorities. This hysteria continued for centuries culminating in the famous Salem trials in America in 1692. Incredibly, similar hysterical behaviour even surfaced at the beginning of the 21st century, when children were killed in London on suspicion of witchcraft and a priest in Romania accused a young nun of being a witch and crucified her. His reasoning was that he was doing God's work.

The common thread throughout history has been the notion that God's work was being done. In truth, rational modern thought would regard all such acts, including those of Henry VIII, Mary Tudor and successive legal authorities, as murder. Open opposition of the Catholic faith was dangerous and would, therefore, mean certain death. John Kurde knew that in Oxford, bishops like Latimer and Ridley, men of great integrity and importance, were speaking out against Catholic doctrine and he foolishly thought he would follow suit. But in 1555, these men were murdered at Mary's hands and were burned at the stake. Two years later, after persistently speaking out against the, now revived, Doctrine of Transubstantiation, and for refusing to attend Holy Communion in his local parish church, John Kurde was arrested, taken to Northampton and imprisoned in the castle. He was tried in All Saints' church and condemned to death by William Binsley, Chancellor to the Bishop of Peterborough.

On 20th September 1557, by command of Sir Thomas Tresham, Sheriff of Northamptonshire, Kurde was taken to the stone pits, close to the present day Royal Mail headquarters on Barrack Road, and there he was burned at the stake. Standing close by was a staunch Catholic priest called John Rote, vicar of St Giles in the town. He urged Kurde to recant, live and be pardoned. Kurde, with his dying breath cried, 'I have my pardon by Jesus Christ.'

John Kurde was the only martyr of the Marian Persecutions in Northamptonshire. He died in the last year of Mary's reign.

THE MYSTERY OF THE GIRL
IN THE PORTRAIT

———————— ❀ ————————

Great Harrowden, Wellingborough 1889

At the foot of the magnificent staircase in Harrowden
Hall hangs a most beautiful portrait. In most country
houses, huge, dark family portraits take up the honoured
positions on the walls. They hang in heavy gilt frames and,
to the 21st century eye, they lack any personality. They
could be of anyone, they are just family portraits. But this
one is clearly not a typical family portrait, for it is small,
light and seemingly modern. It is of a girl with exotic and
quite beautiful features. She has a remote and distant look in
her eyes – a longing – almost as though she wishes she were
somewhere else, somewhere far, far away. It is somewhat
intriguing, almost mysterious, that a portrait like this should
be found in such grand and staid surroundings, but this is a
house that has known mystery and intrigue for centuries.

Harrowden Hall, two miles from Wellingborough, was
home to Baron Vaux and family from 1461 to 1662. In
1511, the 20-year-old King Henry VIII was entertained here
on several occasions and, 100 years later, James I hunted
here. Then it was successively owned by the Earl of Banbury
and Lord Rockingham. It was here that three Vaux women,
Eliza, Anne and Eleanor lived. They were staunch Catholics
at a time of great political intrigue, and in the year 1605 they

Harrowden Hall.

used their home to entertain a group of men whose names have become legendary in English history. Catesby, Tresham and Throckmorton amongst others. These men were all cousins, all Catholics and all gunpowder plotters! The Hall was one of Northamptonshire's 'safe houses' and Catholics from far and wide, including the plotters, came here at the invitation of Eliza Vaux, to celebrate the Feast of St Luke, a couple of weeks before 'gunpowder day'. The Vaux women knew all about the plans to blow up Parliament and, although were not actual plotters, they did risk their lives for their cause. Eliza and Anne were arrested, imprisoned in the Tower and interrogated. They were released and lived long lives. Surely the portrait is not a modern representation of one of the Vaux women? It hangs at the foot of the stairs amid echoes of English history on a site that has been involved in political intrigue and even revolution and yet the girl in the picture looks peaceful and calm. What would she know of intrigue and revolution? And how many people, I wonder, pass the portrait of that lovely young girl every day of the week and have little or no idea who she is?

I first set eyes on the portrait when I was at the house some time ago. As I went upstairs to the dining room, I failed to notice her captivating eyes, but as I came down again after lunch, I stopped in my tracks, I was transfixed and was drawn to the picture as though by a siren. I had to investigate. No one I spoke to that day had any idea of the girl's identity apart from the name inscribed on a dull brass plate on the frame, partially hidden by an arrangement of dried flowers. But at least I had something to go on. I learned that in 1895 the house was sold by the owner, the Earl Fitzwilliam, and was used as a school for young ladies of quality. And it was with this period that the mystery girl in the portrait is associated.

The school was run to the very highest of standards by a Mrs Sharp. Her girls were handpicked from the finest families in the land and beyond. No doubt she was intrigued and delighted when an important businessman and diplomat, Mr Archibald Scott Cleghorn, made contact to enrol his daughter in her establishment. Detailed checks had been made by him regarding the soundness of the education and the safety of the environment. Either the father was exceptionally pernickety or the girl was extremely delicate. In fact, neither was the case. The child was enrolled and it was agreed that she should begin her schooling on 19th September 1889. The new pupil was to be known as Miss Victoria Cleghorn and she was coming to Wellingborough from London after having made the very long and arduous journey by ship from Hawaii to San Francisco, across America by train to New York, and then on to Liverpool.

Victoria Cleghorn was indeed her name, but it was not the name by which she was known at home in Hawaii. There she was Her Royal Highness Princess Victoria Ka'iulani, and her story is as thrilling and dramatic as any you could imagine.

Ka'iulani was the daughter of Archibald Cleghorn, an Edinburgh born adventurer whose parents had moved to New Zealand and then to Hawaii where they owned a store. When they returned to New Zealand, Archie stayed on looking after the store and subsequently, with a keen eye for business, he opened several more stores on other Hawaiian islands. Gradually he worked his way into Hawaiian society and into royal circles, then, on 22nd September 1870, he married Princess Likelike, sister of King Kamehameha V, and in 1875 Princess Victoria Ka'iulani was born. Naturally, the new princess was to be brought up in the royal household and so she was exposed to the rigours of palace life. She mixed with foreign dignitaries who visited and one of her special friends, who arrived in Hawaii in January 1889, was the great Scottish author Robert Louis Stevenson. He wrote poems about her and told her stories and called her 'the little royal maid'.

The new King Kalakaua was aware that Hawaii, remote as it was, had to keep up with a quickly evolving world thousands of miles away. Princess Victoria Ka'iulani was to be the hope of her people. Because the king had no children and his heir, his sister, was also childless it was expected that Ka'iulani would one day play an important role in Hawaiian life. The king and Robert Louis Stevenson had long and detailed discussion about literature, Britain – and Ka'iulani. It was decided that she should receive an education good enough to equip her for the task that almost certainly lay ahead of her. That meant an English education. On 20th March 1889, a decree was issued. 'I Kalakaua, King of the Hawaiian Islands, do hereby give my consent and approval for my niece, her Royal Highness Princess Victoria Ka'iulani to leave the Hawaiian Islands and proceed to England on, or about, the month of May 1889'.

The princess was desolate. Not only was she being forced to leave her beloved home to travel to a cold, foreign country, but also she was leaving her new-found friend, Stevenson. But go she must.

Miss Sharp was the third principal of Great Harrowden Hall School. She followed Miss Agnes Bartlett and Miss Mortimer Rowden; all were formidable educationists with high ideals and distinguished academic careers behind them. At first, Ka'iulani hated it! As a 14 year-old who had never experienced education with other children, it was strange and difficult for her. She had her step-sister, Annie, with her as a companion, so she was not lonely, but that first winter, with its snow and hard frosts, was something she would never forget.

She was a good student; she learned French and German and excelled at art, sewing and games. She had come from a Christian family and, during Lent 1890, Victoria was confirmed by Bishop Francis Thicknesse in the parish church of All Saints, next door to Harrowden Hall. As a Confirmation present, she received a parcel from Robert Louis Stevenson. It was a copy of his latest novel, *The*

Masters of Ballantrae. He had inscribed the book, 'To my dear friend Ka'iulani, my mouse thinks this is my worst effort yet! Your most devoted and respectful friend, Robert Louis Stevenson'. He and his family had left Hawaii and were by now living on Samoa.

But then suddenly, the intrigue and revolution of English history, that Harrowden Hall had witnessed centuries earlier, visited the Hall one again, only this time, it was not to be written in the annals of English history, but those of a country far, far away.

Soon after her confirmation, Ka'iulani received a telegram which told the most disturbing, astounding, thrilling, terrible news. Her uncle, King Kalakaua had died and his sister, Lili'uokalani had become queen. The queen made a pronouncement on the day of her accession, 'Nobles of my Kingdom: I have called you together to deliberate on a grave matter of state. Article 22 of the Constitution calls upon me to appoint a successor to the throne. I now announce to you Our beloved Niece, her Royal Highness Victoria Kawekiu Lunalilo Kalaninuiahilapalapa Ka'iulani, as my successor to the Throne of the Kingdom, and I hope that your deliberations will lead you to approve of my appointment.'

Suddenly, a young girl at school in heart of England was to face the immense responsibility of becoming a monarch. It was almost too much to bear, but she was greatly encouraged by her friends and by the international press, for the news caused great interest world-wide and even in Wellingborough where the local paper hailed the princess as 'one of kindly and gracious disposition, a favourite everywhere'. Soon after her birthday in October 1898, Ka'iulani's father wrote her a peculiar letter. In it he said, 'be on your guard against certain enemies I do not feel free to name in writing.' It mystified her and meant nothing to her at the time, but she was soon to find out.

Gradually Ka'iulani came to accept her future role. She continued with her studies and the delicate young girl became an educated and capable young lady, fully equipped to become a queen. She had even been given a date on which she was to be received by Queen Victoria in Buckingham Palace. The mantle of responsibility was getting heavier by the day. Then in January 1893 came another telegram, then another, and another. Each brought increasingly worse news. 'Queen Deposed'. 'Monarchy Abrogated'. 'Break news to Princess'.

It seemed that, within a very short space of time, Ka'iulani had gone from being a schoolgirl to an heir apparent of a sovereign throne, to a stateless girl. It was more than she could take. The Hawaiian monarchy had, indeed, been overthrown. Her aunt the queen was deposed and Ka'iulani was, in effect, no longer a royal princess.

John Stevens, the American Minister to Hawaii, had a long-held desire to see the Islands become part of America. Unwittingly helped by a new constitution that was being proposed by Queen Lili'uokalani, that sought to change voting rights amongst native Hawaiians, two rebel cabinet members went to allies of Stevens for advice. Another cabinet faction wanted to replace the queen with Ka'iulani straight away as a constitutional monarch. Still another faction, the most dangerous, wanted to have Hawaii annexed to America. It was inevitable that a coup d'etat of some sort was about to happen. John Stevens landed at Honolulu and soldiers marched up the main street. The queen, fearing for her people, signed a document of resignation and Stevens immediately set up a provisional government.

There was still hope that Ka'iulani could save the day and become queen, but it was a faint hope in reality. The time came for Ka'iulani to leave England. With a guardian and thirteen trunks and nine bags, she set sail for New York on the *Teutonic*. When she arrived in New York, the press turned out in hoards and she made a passionate speech in favour of her nation. So supportive was her audience that Ka'iulani was fired up even more. The next stop would be Washington DC and the President. After he saw the princess, he gave a

Princess Victoria Ka'iulani's portrait at the foot of the stairs, Harrowden Hall (Courtesy Wellingborough Golf Club).

temporary signal of hope by withdrawing the Hawaiian treaty, which was pending. Ka'iulani was the toast of Washington and was invited to receptions and parties and met many influential people. She then left once again for England. Ka'iulani came back to Northamptonshire and arrived in Burton Latimer, near Kettering, where she stayed with her former headmistress, Mrs Sharp. Ka'iulani was now almost penniless since her allowances had been cut off. She grew impatient, but there was little she could do at so great a distance. She travelled to various places in Britain and Europe, but Burton Latimer remained her base, it was just three miles from the school that helped to groom her for monarchy.

After a great deal of political manoeuvres in Hawaii, a declaration was released on 4th July 1894, stating that Hawaii was now a republic. In November 1897, after eight years away, Ka'iulani returned to Hawaii. On 12th August 1898, the Islands were annexed to the United States. The Hawaiian flag was lowered for the last time and the Stars and Stripes, the emblem incidentally, that had its origin at Sulgrave in Northamptonshire, the Washington family home centuries earlier, flew in its place.

On 6th March 1899, Princess Victoria Ka'iulani died peacefully at 'Āinahau', which means 'the cool place'. It was the Royal Palace up in the mountains, an hour from Honolulu, that her father had built for her mother, Princess Likelike on their marriage. Every Hawaiian will tell you that Victoria Ka'iulani died of a broken heart, and who are we to doubt it?

Back in England, where she went to school, the local papers carried a touching obituary headed, 'Death of Wellingborough Princess.' It is little wonder that the portrait at the foot of the stairs in Harrowden Hall shows a beautiful girl with a remote and distant look in her eyes – a longing – almost as though she wishes she were somewhere else, somewhere far, far away.

THE OAK BEDROOM

❖

Althorp 1855 & 1994

As far as tourism is concerned, Northamptonshire remains relatively unknown but, since the marriage and tragic death of Diana, Princess of Wales, more and more people have learned about the county and have visited it. The place most people want to see is Althorp, the place where Diana spent a great deal of her teenage years and where, now, she is buried. It is amazing to think that, way back in 1486, Sir John Spencer leased the land at Althorp from one of the Catesby family and, a little later, he bought it for what must have been something of a king's ransom, £800! Since then, the estate, the house and the family, have rarely been out of the public eye.

Althorp has been home to the Spencer family since 1508. Like all English country seats, its history is bound up with its noble occupants. It is one of the great treasure houses of Europe and contains one of the most famous collections of paintings and *objets d'art* to be seen anywhere. Over the centuries, from John the 1st Earl Spencer to Charles the 9th and present earl, each has stamped his own very personal identity on the place. One earl was a great collector, another carried out extensions and improvements; a later earl assembled a great library, yet another earl sold it! That is the way it goes in families and houses that are the very stuff of English history.

Althorp.

Huge as it is, the house is very much a home. But in the eyes of Charles, the 9th Earl, it has not always been like that. As a boy, during the occupancy of his grandfather, he rarely slept in what he thought was a 'terrifying house'. It was enormous by any standards and, like all children, he must have heard the echoes of footsteps and doors closing, real or imagined, down the long corridors and passages.

But now, with his feet firmly on the ground, Earl Spencer has little truck with things that go bump in the night! Althorp really is a family home and, although guests may not be used to such surroundings, few feel intimidated. That feeling of friendship and welcome is due entirely to the present occupants, Charles and Caroline. They lead busy lives in London and yet, Althorp is still their home at weekends. And at Christmas and during holidays, it can be teeming with children, scooting, running, or 'rug-tobogganing' on the polished floors. It may come as a shock to weekend guests when they realise that they will actually be sleeping in one of the state rooms; in the same beds that had been occupied by the great and the good over the centuries.

The oak bedroom is one of those breathtaking rooms still used regularly by Earl Spencer's youthful visitors. It is a large room, of course, and very grand. The deep red walls are hung with magnificent portraits and the room is opulently furnished. A Boulle writing table stands at the foot of a big four-poster bed, the bed hangings of which are of heavy blue velvet embroidered with gold coronets and the 'S' motif. It is a room that was, many years ago, the scene of a great romance.

It was in this room in 1755 that John 1st Earl Spencer married his sweetheart in deadly secret. The object of his love was Georgiana Poyntz. This was no arranged marriage; it was a case of true love. The marriage was set for Christmas day, as a finale to John's 21st birthday celebrations, and things were planned on an epic scale. The whole neighbourhood was involved with opulence rarely matched anywhere. 5,000 people had gathered in nearby Great Brington, and between them they downed 11,000 pints of beer before nightfall, a feat to be repeated the next day!

The marriage licence arrived to authorise the nuptials, but John was impatient and went to Georgiana and suggested that, like a Judy Garland/Mickey Rooney musical, they marry, right here, right now!

And so it was. The principal guests were smuggled out of the ballroom and gathered in the oak bedroom, which was being used by John's mother at the time. John's tutor was also a clergyman and he sneaked away from the dancing to perform the rite. After the knot was tied, the wedding party returned to the picture gallery and no one was any the wiser!

Many present day guests may enjoy sampling those romantic associations endowed upon the oak bedroom by John and Georgiana but, to sleep in a room with more mysterious associations may not be so appealing: for the oak bedroom has a ghost.

Many great houses, and some small ones, are said to have ghosts. It is part of their appeal and romance. After all, if you cannot claim that 'Queen Elizabeth Slept Here', then a ghost gives a house the kind of credibility that the tourist trade likes! Some ghosts are famous and have great stories built around them, others, like the ghost at Althorp, have not been widely recorded and have appeared rarely.

One day in 1994, Charles Spencer was in Althorp's beautiful library. His eye had landed upon a book with a red leather spine. He had never seen the book before, let alone opened it. It was a collection of press-cuttings assembled by his great-great-great grandfather, Frederick, 4th Earl Spencer, known as Fritz. One particular cutting caught Charles Spencer's attention and he perched on the step-ladder and read it with interest. The cutting was from a gossip column diary in a London newspaper and was an

The Oak bedroom (© Althorp).

account of an Althorp house party given by Earl 'Fritz' for a group of worthies of the time. Althorp in the 1850s was alive with guests and, of course, with staff to look after them. There were 25 categories of staff on the estate and in the house, from housekeeper to parlour maid, butler to groom and everything in between. The house itself would have had around 65 full-time staff, an incredible number of employees, but then Althorp is an incredible house.

One of the guests on that particular weekend was the Dean of Lincoln, The Very Reverend John Giffard Ward, who was to sleep in the oak bedroom, situated on the first floor, immediately off the Spencer picture gallery that overlooks the vast saloon. One morning during the weekend, Dean Ward came down for breakfast in a rather disagreeable humour. He had retired at the same time as the family and the rest of the guests but, during the night, he had been disturbed by an intruder. His host was, naturally, concerned and asked the Dean what had happened so that he could have the matter investigated. The Dean explained that during the night he had been woken by a man who appeared, by the uniform he was wearing, to be a groom. As he adjusted to the inconvenient interruption to his sleep, he saw that the groom was carrying a large candelabrum and was going round the bed and the room checking that all the other candles had been extinguished. The groom disappeared and the Dean, with some apprehension, returned to his ecclesiastical slumbers.

His account was met with silence from the family. Then someone asked the Dean if he would kindly describe the groom in more detail. This he did and, to everyone's surprise, the description matched exactly the favourite groom of the 3rd Earl, John Charles, Fritz's brother. It was well known to the family that the groom had been given a very responsible task. Each night, after everyone had retired, he was to go round the house and into all the rooms, to check that all candles had been snuffed out. The spirit of the groom had obviously continued to do this on the very night that the Dean had slept in the room.

The story amused, rather than alarmed, the 9th Earl and he replaced the red leather book and, realising that he too had guests arriving for the weekend, he set off to see to arrangements. The weekend went well and his friends spent a happy couple of days at Althorp. On Sunday evening, he bid his guests farewell having, as usual, helped them with their bags and baggage. Just as Charles Spencer was helping a young girl to carry her luggage from her bedroom, she turned to him and said something that made him stop in his tracks. He put her bags down and listened as she made the most amazing remark. 'Do you know, I swear that someone came in here last night.' Lord Spencer's immediate reaction was to dismiss it, because it was quite possible that someone had gone to the wrong room late at night. But suddenly, his attitude changed. 'And the strange thing is,' she continued, 'he was holding a candelabrum and was wearing an old uniform – a cloak.'

Immediately Charles thought back to his strange discovery of a couple of days earlier in the library. The account in the book of press-cuttings about the Dean and his nocturnal supernatural visitor. 'Hang on,' Charles Spencer said, and he ran to another part of the house where his housekeeper, Joyce Coles, had assembled a whole range of items ready for a small display in one of the stables. Among these were various uniforms from a former age that had been hidden away in unvisited rooms for many a long year. He picked up a groom's cloak intending to take it down to show to his guest. But he stopped and instead chose a footman's uniform that was nothing like the groom's cloak. He was turning the episode into something of a game. He ran down the stairs and breathlessly offered the uniform to his guest and asked her if it resembled the garb worn by her mysterious visitor.

'Almost,' she said fingering the musty cloth, 'but it was longer and …'. She described in precise detail the costume that lay upstairs, waiting to be put on show in the new museum. The uniform of a groom dating from around 1850.

The girl had been sleeping in the oak bedroom.